A SIMPLE GUIDE TO SPOKEN TAMIL
THROUGH ENGLISH (Revised Version)

ALOYSIUS ASEERVATHAM

2023

Gotham Books

30 N Gould St.
Ste. 20820, Sheridan, WY 82801
https://gothambooksinc.com/

Phone: 1 (307) 464-7800

© 2023 *Aloysius Aseervatham*. All rights reserved.

No part of this book may be reproduced, stored in a retrieval system, or transmitted by any means without the written permission of the author.

Published by Gotham Books (April 26, 2023)

ISBN: 979-8-88775-100-9 (P)
ISBN: 979-8-88775-101-6 (E)

Because of the dynamic nature of the Internet, any web addresses or links contained in this book may have changed since publication and may no longer be valid.

The views expressed in this work are solely those of the author and do not necessarily reflect the views of the publisher, and the publisher hereby disclaims any responsibility for them.

TABLE OF CONTENTS

- LESSON 1 - TAMIL VOWELS 16
- LESSON 2 - TAMIL CONSONANTS 18
- LESSON 3 - SIMILAR SOUNDING ALPHABETS 22
- LESSON 4 - SALIENT ASPECTS OF TAMIL 24
- LESSON 5 – LEARNING TAMIL USING ENGLISH 32
- LESSON 6 - THE FIRST, SECOND & THIRD PERSONS – (1) . 35
- LESSON 7 - THE FIRST, SECOND & THIRD PERSONS – (2) . 38
- LESSON 8 – QUERY WORDS – (1) 40
- LESSON 9 – QUERY WORDS – (2) 42
- LESSON 10 - HUMAN BODY PARTS – (1)................................... 44
- LESSON 11 - HUMAN BODY PARTS – (2)................................... 46
- LESSON 12 - HUMAN BODY PARTS – (3)................................... 47
- LESSON 13 - HUMAN BODY PARTS - (4) 50
- LESSON 14 - HUMAN BODY PARTS – (5)................................... 51
- LESSON 15 - HOUSEHOLD ITEMS.. 53
- LESSON 16 - COLOURS 55
- LESSON 17 - GREETINGS & SALUTATIONS............................. 57
- LESSON 18 - COMMANDS.. 59
- LESSON 19 - DIRECTIONS 61
- LESSON 20 - RELATIVES – (1) 63
- LESSON 21 - RELATIVES – (2) 65
- LESSON 22 - RELATIVES - (3) 67
- LESSON 23 - AT THE POST OFFICE 69
- LESSON 24 - AROUND THE HOUSE/ HOTEL 71
- LESSON 25 - COUNTING – (1)... 73

LESSON 26 - COUNTING – (2)	75
LESSON 27 - COUNTING – (3)	77
LESSON 28 - COUNTING – (4)	79
LESSON 29 - COUNTING – (5)	81
LESSON 30 - COUNTING – (6)	83
LESSON 31 - PLACE COUNTING	85
LESSON 32 - TELLING THE TIME	87
LESSON 33 - COMMON WORDS	89
LESSON 34 - MONTHS OF THE YEAR	91
LESSON 35 - DAYS OF THE WEEK	93
LESSON 36 - WORKERS	95
LESSON 37 - EVILS	97
LESSON 38 – CREATURES – (1)	99
LESSON 39 – CREATURES – (2)	101
LESSON 40 - CREATURES - (3)	103
LESSON 41 - CROCKERY	105
LESSON 42 - VEGETABLES	107
LESSON 43 - FRUITS	109
LESSON 44 - SEAFOOD	111
LESSON 45 - MEATS	113
LESSON 46 - STATIONERY	115
LESSON 47 - MONEY DEALINGS	117
LESSON 48 - INSTITUTIONS/ BUILDINGS	119
LESSON 49 - MODES OF TRANSPORT	121
LESSON 50 - LOCATIONS	123
LESSON 51 - GARDENS/ VEGETATION	125
LESSON 52 - SPICES	127
LESSON 53 - PERSONS	129
LESSON 54 - OFFICE ACCESSORIES	131

LESSON 55 - RATES OF MOTION 133
LESSON 56 - CONVERSATION - 1 135
LESSON 57 - CONVERSATION - 2 136
LESSON 58 - CONVERSATION - 3 137
LESSON 59 - CONVERSATION - 4 138
LESSON 60 - CONVERSATION - 5 140
LESSON 61 - CONVERSATION - 6 142
LESSON 62 - CONVERSATION - 7 144
LESSON 63 - CONVERSATION - 8 145
LESSON 64 - CONVERSATION - 9 145
LESSON 65 - CONVERSATION -10 149
LESSON 66 - CONVERSATION -11 150
LESSON 67 - CONVERSATION -12 152
ANSWERS TO EXERCISES 155
ADDITIONAL VOCABULARY 179

DEDICATION

This book is dedicated to the living and loving memory of my parents Mr. and Mrs. M.V. Aseervatham

FOREWORD

I am lucky to have had a sound education in Tamil language during my school days. My father who was a Tamil scholar and an author helped me greatly in this respect. As a result, I am able to use my Tamil knowledge to write this book.

In 2011, I had a desire to write a basic book for anybody interested in learning the Tamil language and so, I published a book titled "A Simple Guide to Spoken Tamil".

This book "A Simple Guide to Spoken Tamil", a revised version would be very useful to anyone wishing to learn to speak as well as write the Tamil Language with ease.

The book focuses on the mastery of 'essential' Tamil vocabulary and their usage in sentences. Once this basic knowledge is obtained the reader can confidently embark on a more advanced study of this language.

Aloysius Aseervatham

Brisbane – Australia   April 2023

ACKNOWLEDGEMENTS

Twelve years ago, in 2011 when this book was first written, a few of my close associates helped to perfect it.

Ratnam Kandasamy of Melbourne and Caroline Thurairatnam of Sydney helped me with the production of physical audio to assist the learner with the Tamil pronunciation. However, this new version of the book has access to audio files via the author's website: **www.aseervathambooks.com**

This revised version with additional features, especially the inclusion of additional exercises was made easy with the able assistance of my granddaughter **Zuleikha Aseervatham,** a graduate of the University of Queensland. I greatly admire her continued dedication to help her grandfather with his passion for writing self-help books.

AA

INTRODUCTION

This revised edition of "A Simple Guide to Spoken Tamil" has a few helpful additional exercises included to help speed up the learning process!

Lessons 1 and 2 cover the Tamil vowels and consonants and their mastery will lead to learning and understanding the common Tamil words used in conversations.

Lessons 3 and 4 give an insight into the nature of the Tamil language and Lesson 5 looks at some simple phrases.

Each of lessons 6 to 55 is structured in a way to help the reader to learn some cardinal words under a specific category. For example, the lesson on describing colours in Tamil is under "Colours".

Every time a new word is learned in a lesson, it is shown how it is used in a sentence. Other new words get introduced into the sentence. For example, if 'Yellow' is a specific word, the sentence, 'It is a *beautiful* yellow *flower*' introduces two new words.

The reader is encouraged to study the new words presented in each lesson and then test whether they know the exact meaning of those words by doing the simple exercise that is given at the end of each lesson. They are also encouraged to write the Tamil words and sentences using the Tamil script. Failing to identify the correct Tamil meaning of English words given in exercises shouldn't cause any concern as the answers are given for them at the back of the book.

LESSON 1
Tamil Vowels

There are vowels in Tamil as in any other language. We shall look at the twelve vowels in Tamil. A vowel has both a short sound and a long sound. It is important to know the difference.

We focus on the spoken language. We shall learn the sounds of the **12** Tamil vowels through English in this lesson.

In order to know the exact sound of each vowel, it is recommended that the reader recognises the Tamil script it refers to. It is time well spent learning to recognise the script and even to write it. It helps to pronounce the Tamil words properly. Learning to write, the beautiful Tamil scripts, can be fun indeed!

The twelve Tamil vowels:

அ	ஆ	இ	ஈ	உ	ஊ	எ	ஏ	ஐ	ஒ	ஓ	ஔ
a	aa	iy	iiy	u	uu	e	eh	ai	o	oh	aw

அ	a	(sound for 'a' is as for 'u' in **cup**)
ஆ	aa	(sound for 'aa' is as for 'a' in **car**)
இ	iy	(sound for 'iy' is as for 'ea' in **sea**)
ஈ	iiy	(sound for 'iiy' is as for 'ee' in **free**)
உ	u	(sound for 'u' is as for 'u' in **pull**)

ஊ   uu   (sound for 'uu' is as for 'oo' in **pool**)

எ   e   (sound for 'e' is as for 'e' in egg**)**

ஏ   eh   (sound for 'eh' is as for 'a' in graze)

ஐ   ai   (sound for 'ai' is as for 'i' in k**i**te)

ஒ   o   (sound for 'o' is as for 'o' in **o**nly)

ஓ   oh   (sound for 'oh' is as for 'o' in **o**pen)

ஔ   aw   (Sound for 'aw' is as for 'ou' in pl**ou**gh)

EXERCISE 1:

1. Practice pronouncing the 12 vowels learned in this lesson.

2. Practice writing each Tamil Vowel five times.

3. Listen to a video or YouTube (on your computer) to confirm the pronunciation

4. Practice writing the vowels to understand the differences between short sounding and long sounding vowels. Say them out loud as you write.

LESSON 2
Tamil Consonants

This lesson introduces the 18 consonants in the Tamil language.

In order to know the exact sound of each consonant, it is recommended that the reader recognises, as in the case of vowels, the Tamil character for each consonant. A mastery of the proper sounds will come with talking practice and listening to the audio file.
(Refer www.aseervathambooks.com)

Eighteen Tamil consonants:

க்	ங்	ச்	ஞ்	ட்	ண்	த்	ந்	ப்	ம்	ய்	ர்
ik	ing	ich	inj	idd	inh	ith	inth	ip	im	iy	ir

ல்	வ்	ழ்	ள்	ற்	ன்
il	iv	izh	i<u>ll</u>	itr	in

The consonant க் combines with each of the vowels giving twelve different sounds.

க் + அ	= க	ik + a	= ka
க் + ஆ	= கா	ik + aa	= kaa
க் + இ	= கி	ik + iy	= kiy
க் + ஈ	= கீ	ik + iiy	= kiiy

க் + உ	= கு	ik + u	= ku
க் + ஊ	= கூ	ik + uu	= kuu
க் + எ	= கெ	ik + e	= ke
க் + ஏ	= கே	ik + eh	= keh
க் + ஐ	= கை	ik + ai	= kai
க் + ஒ	= கொ	ik + o	= ko
க் + ஓ	= கோ	ik + oh	= koh
க் + ஔ	= கௌ	ik + aw	= kaw

Note:

There are no Tamil alphabets with sounds "ga" and "ha". The substitute for these sounds will be learned in later lessons.

Note also, there is no Tamil alphabet with the sound 'ba'.

EXERCISE 2a:

1. Say aloud the 18 Tamil consonants, ten times each.

2. Say aloud the 216 **combined** Tamil consonants in the list on the next page, ten times each.

A LIST OF COMBINED CONSONANTS

	அ a	ஆ aa	இ i	ஈ iiy	உ u	ஊ uu	எ e	ஏ ee	ஐ ay	ஒ o	ஓ oh	ஔ aw
க்	க ka	கா kaa	கி ki	கீ kii	கு ku	கூ kuu	கெ ke	கே kay	கை kai	கொ ko	கோ koh	கௌ kaw
ங்	ங nga	ஙா ngaa	ஙி ngi	ஙீ ngii	ஙு ngu	ஙூ nguu	ஙெ nge	ஙே ngay	ஙை ngai	ஙொ ngo	ஙோ ngoh	ஙௌ ngaw
ச்	ச cha	சா chaa	சி chi	சீ chii	சு chu	சூ chuu	செ che	சே chey	சை chai	சொ cho	சோ choh	சௌ chaw
ஞ்	ஞ gna	ஞா gnaa	ஞி gni	ஞீ gnii	ஞு gnu	ஞூ gnuu	ஞெ gne	ஞே gnee	ஞை gnai	ஞொ gno	ஞோ gnoh	ஞௌ gnaw
ட்	ட da	டா daa	டி di	டீ dii	டு du	டூ duu	டெ de	டே dey	டை dai	டொ do	டோ doh	டௌ daw
ண்	ண nha	ணா nhaa	ணி nhi	ணீ nhii	ணு nhu	ணூ nhuu	ணெ nhe	ணே nheh	ணை nhai	ணொ nho	ணோ nhoh	ணௌ nhaw
த்	த tha	தா thaa	தி thi	தீ thii	து thu	தூ thuu	தெ the	தே theh	தை thai	தொ tho	தோ thoh	தௌ thaw
ந் (inth)	ந n	நா na	நி ni	நீ nii	நு nu	நூ nuu	நெ ne	நே neh	நை nai	நொ no	நோ noh	நௌ naw
ப்	ப pa	பா paa	பி pi	பீ pii	பு pu	பூ puu	பெ pe	பே peh	பை pai	பொ po	போ poh	பௌ paw
ம்	ம ma	மா maa	மி mi	மீ mii	மு mu	மூ muu	மெ me	மே meh	மை mai	மொ mo	மோ moh	மௌ maw
ய்	ய ya	யா yaa	யி yi	யீ yii	யு yu	யூ yuu	யெ ye	யே yeh	யை yai	யொ yo	யோ yoh	யௌ yaw
ர்	ர ta	ரா taa	ரி ti	ரீ tii	ரு tu	ரூ tuu	ரெ te	ரே teh	ரை tai	ரொ to	ரோ toh	ரௌ taw
ல்	ல la	லா laa	லி li	லீ lii	லு lu	லூ luu	லெ le	லே leh	லை lai	லொ lo	லோ loh	லௌ law
வ்	வ va	வா vaa	வி vi	வீ vii	வு vu	வூ vuu	வெ ve	வே veh	வை vai	வொ vo	வோ voh	வௌ vaw
ழ்	ழ zha	ழா zhaa	ழி zhi	ழீ zhii	ழு zhu	ழூ zhuu	ழெ zhe	ழே lzheh	ழை zhi	ழொ zho	ழோ zhoh	ழௌ zhaw
ள்	ள lla	ளா llaa	ளி lli	ளீ llii	ளு llu	ளூ lluu	ளெ lle	ளே lleh	ளை llai	ளொ llo	ளோ lloh	ளௌ llaw
ற்	ற ra	றா raa	றி ri	றீ rii	று ru	றூ ruu	றெ re	றே reh	றை rai	றொ ro	றோ roh	றௌ raw
ன்	ன n	னா na	னி ni	னீ ni	னு nu	னூ nuu	னெ ne	னே neh	னை nai	னொ no	னோ noh	னௌ naw

Each consonant has an inherent vowel; the sound can change when combined with different vowels.

THREE TYPES OF COMBINED CONSONANTS

1. Hard sounding: க, ச, ட, த, ப, ற
2. Medium sounding: ங, ஞ, ண, ந, ம, ன
3. Soft sounding: ய, ர, ல, வ, ழ, ள

EXERCISE 2b:

Practise writing and pronouncing each of the combined consonants giving attention to the short and long sounds.

NOTE:

There is no letter in English for the sound of alphabet "ழ". So, our language name is erroneously written as Tamil.

People use "zha" to give the sound of "ழ" and

"izh" for the sound of "ழ்"

If "ழ்" is pronounced by using "izh", then the correct spelling is "**Thamizh**" for our Tamil language.

LESSON 3

Similar Sounding Alphabets

There are some similar sounding alphabets. Their wrong usage in a word would either make the word sound funny or give a totally different meaning.

     ல la
     ள lla
     ழ zha

Examples: The Tamil word for '**flower**' is மலர் ('malar') and not மளர் ('mallar') **or** மழர் ('Mazhar')

    The Tamil word for '**fruit**' is பழம் ('pazham') and **not** பலம் or பளம்.

ர soft r (pronounced 'ta')
ற hard r (pronounced 'ra')

Example: The Tamil word for '**tree**' is matam (மரம்) and **not** மறம் ('maram') which means 'religion'

Note that a word ending with an 'r' sound is written with just 'r' or 'ir' depending on the word.

Example: 'Life' in Tamil is உயிர் ('uyir') and is written with 'ir' at the end.
    Flower in Tamil is மலர் ('malar') and is written with just an 'r' at the end.

22

நௌ　<u>n</u>a
ன　na
ண　nha

For example, Money or பணம் ('panham') is spelt with ண ('nha') and **not** with ன ('na') or ந ('<u>n</u>a')

The Tamil word for **'married person'** is மணமானவர் ('Manhamaanavar') has the sound of both 'nha' and 'na'.

The Tamil word for **'decent person'** is நாணயமானவர் ('<u>n</u>aanhayamaanavar') and has all three sounds <u>n</u>a, na and nha.

EXERCISE 3:

1. Learn to recognise each Tamil alphabet encountered in this lesson from its pronunciation.

2. The Tamil words **moolai** and **moo<u>l</u>lai** mean 'corner' and 'brain' respectively. Write these Tamil words using Tamil script.

3. Differentiate each set of letters below by pronouncing them properly:

   (a) ல, ழ and ள
   　　la　zha　<u>l</u>la

   (b) ர and ற
   　　ta　ra

   (c) ந, ண and ன
   　　<u>n</u>a　nha　na

LESSON 4

Salient Aspects of Tamil

An English sentence does not get translated to Tamil, word to word. Some English words do not get translated but most English words have direct Tamil equivalents. The order of Tamil words may be changed in certain sentences.

How are you?	neenka<u>ll</u>	eppadi	irukkireerka<u>ll</u>?*
	You	*how*	*keeping?*
	நீங்கள்	எப்படி	இருக்கிறீர்கள்?

*Note: In the word 'irukkireerka<u>ll</u>', the combined consonant '**ka**' is pronounced as '**ha**'.

What is your name?	unka<u>ll</u>udaiya,	peyar	enna?
	Your	*name*	*what?*
	உங்களுடைய	பெயர்	என்ன?

Where do you live now?	neenka<u>ll</u>	ippa	enkeh	vasikkireerka<u>ll</u>?
	You	*now*	*where*	*live?*
	நீங்கள்	இப்ப	எங்கே	வசிக்கிறீர்கள்?

How many children do you have?	unka<u>ll</u>ukku	eththanai	Pi<u>ll</u> llai ka<u>ll</u>?
	For you,	*how many*	*children?*
	உங்களுக்கு	எத்தனை	பிள்ளைகள்?

This is a good book	ithu	oru	Nal-la	puththakam.
	This	*one*	*good*	*book.*
	இது	ஒரு	நல்ல	புத்தகம்

Do you want anything else, sir?	unka<u>ll</u>ukku	vehru	ehthaavathu	vehnumaa	aiyaa?
	For you,	*else*	*anything*	*want*	*sir?*
	உங்களுக்கு	வேறு	ஏதாவது	வேணுமா	ஐயா

I must go now	naan	ippa	poha	vehnhum.
	I	*now*	*go*	*must.*
	நான்	இப்ப	போக	வேணும்

Plural words

A few letters get added to the singular word to give the plural word.

	Singular		Plural
bird	Paravai பறவை	**birds**	Paravaika<u>ll</u> பறவைகள்
cat	Poonai பூனை	**cats**	Poonaika<u>ll</u> பூனைகள்
dog	Naai நாய்	**dogs**	Naaika<u>ll</u> நாய்கள்
elephant	Yaanai யானை	**elephants**	Yaanaika<u>ll</u> யானைகள்

monkey	Kuranku குரங்கு	**monkeys**	Kurankuka<u>ll</u>* குரங்குகள்
snake	Paampu பாம்பு	**snakes**	Paampuka<u>ll</u> பாம்புகள்
flower	Malar மலர்	**flowers**	Malarka<u>ll</u> மலர்கள்
book	Puththakam புத்தகம்	**books**	Puththakanka<u>ll</u> புத்தகங்கள்

Note that the italised 'ka' is pronounced 'ha'!

Wrong use of short and long vowel sounds changes the meaning of a word.

Examples:

Thaanam   –   Alms giving   (தானம்)
Thanam   –   Wealth   (தனம்)

Paalam   –   Bridge   (பாலம்)
Palam   –   Strength   (பலம்)

Maalai   –   Necklace **or** evening (மாலை)
Malai   –   Mountain   (மலை)

Wrong use of double consonant changes the meaning of a word.

Examples:

Pu<u>ll</u>y	–	Sour	(புளி)
Puli	–	Tiger	(புலி)

Sothi	–	gravy	(சொதி)
Soththi	–	lame	(சொத்தி)

Sati	–	correct	(சரி)
Saari (or sari)	–	Indian women dress	(சாறி)

Action words have specific endings. Some common endings are:

1. seykiraar   (doing)   e.g., Avar vehlai seykiraar
 செய்கிறார்   (He is doing work)

2. itukkiraar   (sitting)   e.g., Avar kathiraiyil itukkiraar
 இருக்கிறார்   (He is sitting on a chair)

3. kehdkiraar (listening) e.g., Avar el-laaththaiyum kehdkiraar
 கேட்கிறார்   (He is listening to everything)

4. paadukiraar (singing)   e.g., Avar paaddu-p-paadukiraar
 பாடுகிறார்   (He is singing song)

5. adikkiraar   (beating)   e.g., Avar meh<u>ll</u>am adikkiraar
 அடிக்கிறார்   (He is beating a drum)

itukkirathu and itukkiraar are two common endings that indicate the presence, possession or existence of something or someone respectively:

Examples:

I have a book.	ennidam oru puththaham irukkirathu. என்னிடம் ஒரு புத்தகம் இருக்கிறது.
My father is here.	ennaudaiya appah inkeh irukkiraar. என்னுடைய அப்பா இங்கே இருக்கிறார்.

Present and past tenses

Observe the following carefully:

Present tense		Past tense	
I am asking	naan kehdkirehn நான் கேட்கிறேன்	I asked	naan kehddehn நான் கேட்டேன்
I am bathing	naan kulikkirehn நான் குளிக்கிறேன்	I bathed	naan kuliththehn நான் குளித்தேன்
I am bringing	naan konduvaruhirehn நான் கொண்டுவருகிறேன்	I brought	naan konduvanthehn நான் கொண்டுவந்தேன்
I am crying	naan azhukirehn நான் அழுகிறேன்	I cried	naan azhuthehn நான் அழுதேன்
I am coming	naan varuhirehn நான் வருகிறேன்	I came	naan vanthehn நான் வந்தேன்
I am drinking	naan kudikkirehn நான் குடிக்கிறேன்	I drank	naan kudiththehn நான் குடித்தேன்
I am eating	naan saapidukirehn நான் சாப்பிடுகிறேன்	I ate	naan saappiddehn நான் சாப்பிட்டேன்
I am giving	naan kodukkirehn நான் கொடுக்கிறேன்	I gave	naan koduththehn நான் கொடுத்தேன்

I am looking	naan paarkkirehn நான் பார்க்கிறேன்	I looked	naan paarththehn நான் பார்த்தேன்
I am waiting	naan kaaththirukkirehn நான் காத்திருக்கிறேன்	I waited	naan kaaththirunththehn நான் காத்திருந்தேன்

Present, Past and future tenses

Study the following examples carefully:

I speak	naan kathaikkirehn/pehsuhirehn நான் கதைக்கிறேன் / பேசுகிறேன்
I spoke	naan kathaiththehn/pehsinehn நான் கதைத்தேன் / பேசினேன்
I will speak	naan kathaippehn/pehsuvehn நான் கதைப்பேன் / பேசுவேன்
I love her	naan avallai kaathalikkirehn நான் அவளைக் காதலிக்கிறேன்
I loved her	naan avallai kaathaliththehn நான் அவளைக் காதலித்தேன்
I will love her	naan avallai kaathalippehn நான் அவளைக் காதலிப்பேன்
I am riding a bicycle	naan 'cycle' ohdukirehn நான் 'சைக்கிள்' ஓடுகிறேன்
I rode a bicycle	naan 'cycle' ohdinehn நான் 'சைக்கிள்' ஓடினேன்
I will ride a bicycle	naan 'cycle' ohduvehn நான் 'சைக்கிள்' ஓடுவேன்

Query words

Most query words end with "aa".

Examples:

Enna?	(What?)
Unkalukku vehnumaa?	(Do you want?)
Unkalidam irukkirathaa?	(Have you got?)
Unkalukku villankukirathaa?	(Do you understand?)
Appadiyaa?	(Is that so?)

Mixing English words in conversation

Modern spoken Tamil includes English words. It is sometimes convenient to use an English word instead of Tamil word when speaking.

Examples:

'car' onru	(one car)
antha 'market'	(that market)
'supermarket' onrila	(in a supermarket)
'airport' ikku	(to the airport)
'Office' ikku	(to the office)

Using alphabets interchangeably

"**s**" is used instead of '**ch**' depending on the way a Tamil word is commonly pronounced.

Example:

The Tamil word for 'cock' is 'சேவல்' and may be written as 'chehval' or sehval. 'sehval' is the common pronunciation.

'Similarly, 'h' and ''k' can be used interchangeably.

Example:

The Tamil word for 'students' is 'மாணவர்கள்' and may be written as 'maanhavarka<u>ll</u>' or 'maanhavarha<u>ll</u>'. ('ka' is pronounced 'ha')

Note: (i) A Tamil word can have different meanings. The meaning relevant to the sentence in question is the one that is given in this book.

Similarly, different Tamil words can have the same meaning.

Note: (ii) 'tu' is used for the sound 'நு'
  'eh' is used to emphasise the long sound 'ஏ'
  e.g. Kehddehn (கேட்டேன்)

EXERCISE 4:

1. Familiarise yourself with all the new Tamil words encountered in this lesson.

2. Read aloud the following Tamil words and write each word using the Tamil scripts.

(i) ku<u>ll</u>iththehn (ii) itukkirathaa
(iii) konduvatuhirehn (iv) vi<u>ll</u>angkukirathaa
(v) kaathaliththehn

31

LESSON 5
Learning Tamil Using English

In this lesson, we learn to say in Tamil some common everyday phrases using the English alphabet, moving from small sentences to lengthy ones. From the next lesson onwards, in each lesson we first learn the Tamil equivalents of a few English words under a specific category and then learn to say sentences in Tamil involving those words.

Simple common everyday phrases:

1. **I am coming**
   naan varuhirehn.

2. **You come**
   neenka_ll_ vaarunka_ll._

3. **Come this way -**
   inthapakkam vaarunka_ll_

4. **May I come in?**
   naan ullukku varalaamaa?

5. **Have you eaten?**
   neenka_ll_ saappiddeerha_ll_aa?

6. **Will you come?**
   neenka_ll_ varuveerha_ll_aa?

7. **That bus is big**
   antha 'bus' perisu.

8. **My elder brother is coming tomorrow**
   ennudaiya annan naa_ll_aikku varuhiraar

9. **I want to go now**
   naan ippa pohha vehnum

10. **Give me something**
    enakku ehthaavathu thaarunka<u>ll</u>

11. **What else do you want?**
    unka<u>ll</u>ukku vehru enna vehnum?

12. **Why can't you come?**
    neenka<u>ll</u> ehn vara mudiyaathu?

13. **We are planning to go next Sunday**
    naanka<u>ll</u> aduththa "Sunday' poha yohsikkirohm.

14. **To what places will you go?**
    neenka<u>ll</u> entha idanka<u>ll</u>ukku pohveerha<u>ll</u>?

15. **He is coming at eight o'clock**
    avar eddu manikku varuvaar

16. **I will be going around seven o'clock in the morning**
    naan kaalai ehzhu mani pohla pohvehn

17. **I get good income from that job.**
    enakku antha vehlaiyil irunthu nal-la varumaanam kidaikkirathu

18. **What other languages does that gentleman know other than Tamil?**
    avarukku thamizhai vida vehru enna paasaiha<u>ll</u> theriyum?

19. **Do you have to go anywhere now?**
    neenka<u>ll</u> ippa vehru enkehyaavathu poh-ha vehnuma?

20. **Tomorrow I am going to Kandy or Peradeniya**
naallaikku naan Kandy ikku al-lathu
Perathehniyavukku-p- poh-hirehn

EXERCISE 5:

1. Write the three sentences below using **Tamil scripts**.

    1. Naallaikku enathu pallllikkuuda vidumurai mudikirathu.
    2. Puthu vahuppil padippikka nalla aasitiyarhall vara vehnum.
    3. Thamizh aasitiyar keddikkaarataaka irrukka vehnum.

2. Read each sentence above three times, pronouncing the Tamil words properly.

LESSON 6

The First, Second & Third Persons (1)

I, Me, You, We, They, He, She

English word	Tamil word written using English	Tamil word written using Tamil script
I /Me	naan	நான்
You	nee / neenka<u>ll</u>	நீ / நீங்கள்
We/Us	naanka<u>ll</u> / naam	நாங்கள் / நாம்
They/Them	avarha<u>ll</u>	அவர்கள்
He/She	avar / ava (avan / ava<u>ll</u>)	அவர் / அவ (அவன் / அவள்)

Some action words

English word	Tamil pronunciation using English	Tamil writing
Play	vi<u>ll</u>aiaadu	விளையாடு
Study	padi	படி
Sleep	niththirai sei	நித்திரை செய்
Cry	azhu	அழு
Laugh	siti	சிரி

EXERCISE 6:

Say aloud in Tamil each English sentence given below.

English sentence	Tamil equivalent using English scripts
I am playing.	naan villaiaadukirehn.
I played.	naan villaiaadinehn.
She is playing.	avall villaiaaduhiraall.
He is playing.	avan villaiaaduhiraan.
She played.	avall villaiaadinaall.
He played.	avan villaiaadinaan.
You are playing.	neenkall villaiaaduhireerhall.
You played.	neenkall villaiaadineerhall.
We are playing.	naankall villaiaaduhirohm.
We played.	naankall villaiaadinohm.
They played.	avarhall villaiaadinaarhall.
I am studying.	naan padikkirehn.
I studied.	naan padiththehn.
She is studying.	avall padikkiraall.
He is studying.	avan padikkiraan.
She studied.	avall padiththaall.
He studied.	avan padiththaan.
You are studying.	neenkall padikkireerhall.
You studied.	neenkall padiththeerhall.
We are studying.	naankall padikkirohm.
We studied.	naankall padiththohm.
They are studying.	avarhall padikkiraarhall.
They studied.	avarhall padiththaarhall.
I am laughing.	naan sitikkirehn.
I laughed.	naan sitiththehn.

She laughed.	ava<u>ll</u> sitiththaa<u>ll</u>.
He laughed.	avan sitiththaan.
You laughed.	neenka<u>ll</u> sititheerha<u>ll</u>.
We laughed.	naanka<u>ll</u> sitiththohm.
They laughed.	avarha<u>ll</u> sitiththaarha<u>ll</u>.

LESSON 7

The First, Second & Third Persons (2)

Mine, Your, Our, Us, Him, His, Her, Their, Them

English word	Tamil word written using English	Tamil word written using Tamil script
Mine	ennudaiya	என்னுடைய
Your	ummudaiya unka<u>ll</u>udaiya	உம்முடைய உங்களுடைய
Our	enka<u>ll</u>udaiya	எங்களுடைய
Us	enka<u>ll</u>	எங்கள்
Him	(avar) avan	(அவர்) அவன்
His	avarudaiya / avanudaiya	அவருடைய / அவனுடைய
Her	avavudaiya / ava<u>ll</u>udaiya	அவவுடைய / அவளுடைய
Their	avarha<u>ll</u>udaiya	அவர்களுடைய
Them	avarha<u>ll</u>	அவர்கள்

Say in Tamil, the English sentences given in the first column below:

English sentence	Tamil equivalent using English scripts
That book is mine	athu ennudaiya puththaham
I studied with him	naan avarudan padiththehn
I am his friend	naan avarudaiya sinehkithan
Jayantha is her brother	'Jayantha' avavudaiya sahohtharan
It is your duty	athu unka_ll_udaiya kadamai
It is their home	athu avarhaludaiya veedu
He brought it for us	avar athai enka_ll_ukkuk konduvanthaar
I will go with them	naan avarha_ll_udan pohvehn

EXERCISE 7

1. What are the Tamil words for the following?

    (i) book (ii) friend (iii) brother (iv) duty
    (v) home (vi) brought (vii) will-go

2. Read aloud the Tamil equivalent of each English sentence in the Table above.

LESSON 8
Query Words (1)

Who, When, Where, What, How, How many? How much?

English word	Tamil word written using English	Tamil word written using Tamil script
Who?	yaar?	யார்?
When?	eppa?	எப்ப?
Where?	enkeh?	எங்கே?
What?	enna?	என்ன?
How?	eppadi?	எப்படி?
How many?	eththanai?	எத்தனை?
How much?	evvallavu?	எவ்வளவு?

Say in Tamil the English sentences given in the first column below.

English sentence	Tamil equivalent using English script
Who is he?	yaar avar? (or avar yaar?)
Who is your father?	unka<u>ll</u>udaiya appah yaar?
Who did you meet?	neenka<u>ll</u> yaarai santhiththeerha<u>ll</u>?
Who do you want to meet?	neenka<u>ll</u> yaarai-p-paarkavehnum?
When did that happen?	athu eppa nadanthathu?
When is he coming?	avar eppa varuhiraar?

When are you coming?	neenka_ll_ eppa varuveerha_ll_?
When are you going?	neenka_ll_ eppa pohireerha_ll_?
Where do you live?	neenka_ll_ enkeh vasikkireerha_ll_?
Where does he live?	avar enkeh vasikkiraar?
Where is the temple?	kohvil enkeh irukkirathu?
What is your name?	unka_ll_udaiya peyar enna?
What happened?	enna nadanthathu?
What is your occupation?	unka_ll_udaiya vehlai enna?
What is the problem?	enna pirachchanai?
What time is it now?	ippa nehram enna?
How are you?	eppadi irukkireerha_ll_?
How old are you?	unka_ll_ vayathu enna?
How many children do you have?	unka_ll_ukku eththanai pillaiha_ll_ irukkiraarha_ll_?
How did this happen?	ithu eppadi nadanthathu?
How many people are there?	ankeh eththanai pehr irukkiraarha_ll_?
How much is a kilo of rice?	oru 'kilo' arisi enna vilai?

EXERCISE 8

1. What are the Tamil words for the following?
   (i) father   (ii) live   (iii) temple   (iv) name
   (v) occupation   (vi) problem   (vii) time   (viii) children
   (ix) people.

2. Read aloud the Tamil equivalent of each English sentence in the Table above.

LESSON 9
Query Words (2)

Is it not? Is it true? Is it a female? Is it a male? Do you understand?

English	Tamil equivalent written using English	Tamil equivalent written using Tamil script
Is it not?	appadiththaaneh?	அப்படித்தானே?
Is it true?	athu unhmaiya?	அது உண்மையா?
Is it a female?	athu pehnnaa?	அது பெண்ணா?
Is it a male?	athu aanhaa?	அது ஆணா?
Do you understand?	unka_ll_ukku vi_ll_ankuthaa?	உங்களுக்கு விளங்குதா?

Say in Tamil the English sentences given in the first column below:

English sentence	Tamil equivalent using English script
You are not telling the truth. **Is it not?**	neenka_ll_ unmaiyai sollukireerha_ll_ illai. appadiththaaneh?
I heard that your marriage is next month. **Is it true?**	unka_ll_ vivaaham aduththa maatham enru keh_ll_vippaddehn. athu unhmaiyaa?

Malini had a baby. Is it a female?	Maalinikku kuzhanthai piranthathaam. athu pehnnaa?
Mervyn is adopting a child. Is it a male?	'Mervyn' oru kuzhanthayai thaththu edukkiraartaam. athu aanhaa?
You have to continue to do all what I have told you. Do you understand?	neenka_ll_, naan chonnathu ellavatraiyum thodarnthu seiyavehnum. uunka_ll_ukku vi_ll_ankuthaa?

EXERCISE 9

1. What are the Tamil words for the following?

    (i) truth   (ii) baby   (iii) marriage
    (iv) continue   (v) told   (vi) understand

2. Read aloud the Tamil equivalent of each English sentence in the Table above.

LESSON 10
Human Body Parts (1)

Head, Hair, Forehead, Eye, Ear, Nose

English word	Tamil word written using English	Tamil word written using Tamil script
Head	thalai	தலை
Hair	mayir/mudi	மயிர் / முடி
Forehead	netri	நெற்றி
Eye(s)	kahn(kall)	கண்(கள்)
Ear(s)	kaathu(hall)	காது(கள்)
Nose	muukku	மூக்கு

Say in Tamil the English sentences given in the first column below:

English sentence	Tamil Pronunciation using English
He has shaved his head	avar thanathu thalaiyai vazhiththuviddaar
I have to go for a haircut	naan thalai mudi vedda pohavehnum
She had 'pottu' on her forehead	ava netriyil poddu vaiththirunthaa
Her eyes are very beautiful	ava<u>ll</u>udaiya kahnka<u>ll</u> nal-la vadivu

How is your ear problem now?	unka<u>ll</u> kaathu-p-pitachchanai ippa eppadi?
He has a big nose	avarukku-p-periya muukku

EXERCISE 10

1. What are the Tamil words for the following?

   (i) shave (ii) haircut (iii) beautiful
   (iv) problem (v) big

.2. Read aloud the Tamil equivalent of each English sentence in the Table above.

LESSON 11
Human Body Parts (2)

Mouth, Tooth, Tongue, Chin, Cheek, Neck

English word	Tamil word written using English script	Tamil word written using Tamil script
Mouth	vaayi	வாய்
Tooth (Teeth)	pal (patrka<u>ll</u>)	பல் / பற்கள்
Tongue	naakku	நாக்கு
Chin	naadi	நாடி
Cheek(s)	kannam (kannanka<u>ll</u>) chokkai(ha<u>ll</u>)	கன்னம் / கன்னங்கள் சொக்கை(கள்)
Neck	kazhuththu	கழுத்து

Say in Tamil the English sentences given in the first column below:

English sentence	Tamil equivalent using English script
The child has something in the mouth.	kuzhanthai vaayil ehtoh vaiththirukkirathu.
She brushes her teeth daily.	ava thinamum pal theedduvaa.
Show your tongue.	unka<u>ll</u>udaiya naakkai – k kaaddunka<u>ll</u>.
You have something on your chin.	unka<u>ll</u>udaiya naadiyil ehtoh irukkirathu.

You have a birthmark on your cheek.	unka_ll_udaiya kannaththil pirappu adaiyaa_ll_am onru irukkirathu.
She has a long neck	avavukku kaluththu nee_ll_am.

EXERCISE 11

1. What are the Tamil words for the following?

   (i) child   (ii) something   (iii) brush
   (iv) birthmark   (v) long

2. Read aloud the Tamil equivalent of each English sentence in the Table above.

Key:
1. வாய்
2. பற்கள்
3. நாக்கு
4. நாடி
5. கன்னம்
6. கழுத்து

LESSON 12
Human Body Parts (3)

Nail, Thigh, Leg, Foot, Toe, Finger, Thumb

English word	Tamil word written using English script	Tamil word written using Tamil script.
Nail(s)	naham(nahanka_ll_)	நகம் (நகங்கள்)
Thigh(s)	thodai(ha_ll_)	தொடை(கள்)
Leg(s)	kaal(ha_ll_)	கால்(கள்)
Foot(feet)	paatham(paathanka_ll_)	பாதம் (பாதங்கள்)
Toe(s)	kaal viral(ha_ll_)	கால் விரல்(கள்)
Finger(s)	Kai viral(ha_ll_)	கைவிரல்(கள்)
Thumb(s)	peru viral(ha_ll_)	பெரு விரல்(கள்)

Say in Tamil the English sentences given in the first column below:

English sentence	Tamil equivalent using English script
I am cutting my fingernails	naan enathu kai viral nakankalai veddukirehn.
He has hurt his thigh bone	avar thanathu thodai elumpai thaakki viddaar.
She has long legs	avavukku neenda kaalha_ll_.
You have to take care of your feet	neenka_ll_ unka_ll_udaiya paathankalai kavanikka vehnum.

He had hit his toe against a stone	avar thanathu kaal peru viralai kal-lohdu adiththuviddar
His thumb is swollen	avarudaiya kai-p-peru viral veenkiyu<u>ll</u>athu

EXERCISE 12

1. What are the Tamil words for the following?

   (i) small   (ii) bone   (iii) hurt
   (iv) take care (v) hit   (vi) swollen

2. Read aloud the Tamil equivalent of each English sentence in the Table above.

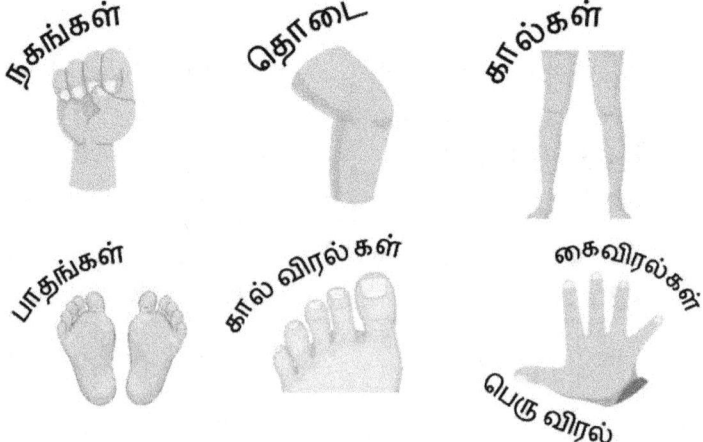

LESSON 13
Human Body Parts (4)

Chest, Breast, Armpit, Back, Bottom

English word	Tamil word written using English script	Tamil word written using Tamil script
Chest	maarpu / nenchu	மார்பு / நெஞ்சு
Breast(s)	mulai(ha<u>ll</u>)	முலை(கள்)
Armpit(s)	kamakkaddu(ha<u>ll</u>)	கமக்கட்டு(கள்)
Back	muthuhu	முதுகு
Bottom	kiizh-p-paaham	கீழ்ப்பாகம்

Say in Tamil the English sentences given in the first column below:

English sentence	Tamil equivalent using English script
He has a chest infection	avarukku nenchila thotru nohyi
She has breast cancer	avavukku mulaiyil putru nohyi
He has a pain in his arm pit	avarukku kamakkaddil oru noh
He has a back problem	avarukku muthuhil oru pirachchanai
His bottom is sore	avarin kiizh-p-pakkaththil noh

EXERCISE 13

1. What are the Tamil words for the following?
   (i) infection (ii) pain (iii) sore (iv) cancer

2. Write each sentence in the table above in Tamil script

50

LESSON 14

Human Body Part (5)

Heart, Liver, Kidney, Stomach, Lung, Womb

English word	Tamil word written using English script	Tamil word written using Tamil script.
Heart	ithayam / iruthayam	இதயம் / இருதயம்
Liver	eeral	ஈரல்
Kidney	siru-neeraham	சிறுநீரகம்
Stomach	vayiru	வயிறு
Lung	nurai-eeral	நுரையீரல்
Womb	utharam	உதரம்

Say in Tamil the English sentences given in the first column below:

English sentence	Tamil equivalent using English script
He is a heart patient	avar oru iruthaya nohyaali
He has liver cancer	avarukku eeralil puttru nohyi
She had stone in the kidney	avavin siru-neerakaththil kal irunthathu
What is wrong with your stomach?	unka__l__ludaiya vayitril enna pizhai
His lungs are weak	avarudaiya nurai-eeralha__ll__ palaveenamaaha irukkinrana
She had a womb operation	avavukku utharaththil saththira sihichchai nadanththathu

51

EXERCISE 14

1. What are the Tamil words for the following?
   (i) patient (ii) stones (iii) wrong (iv) weak
   (v) operation

2. Write each sentence in the table above in Tamil script

3. Match a picture to a word.

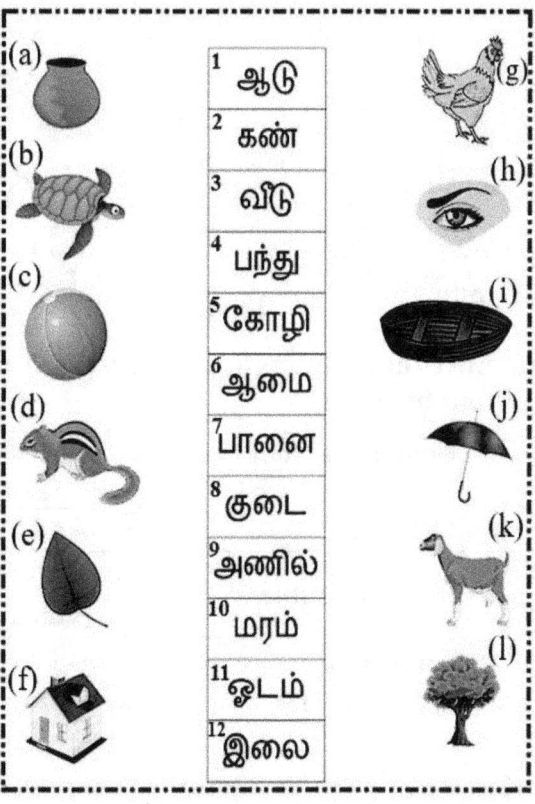

LESSON 15

Household Items

Chair, Table, Bed, Desk, Stool, Bookshelf, Door, Window

English word	Tamil word written using English script	Tamil word written using Tamil script
Chair	kathirai	கதிரை
Table	mehsai	மேசை
Bed	Padukkai / kaddil	படுக்கை / கட்டில்
Desk	ezhuththu mehsai	எழுத்து மேசை
Stool	siru-naatrkaali	சிறு நாற்காலி
Bookshelf	Puththaha-th-thaddu	புத்தகத்தட்டு
Door	kathavu	கதவு
Window	jannal	யன்னல்

Say in Tamil the English sentences given in the first column below:

English sentence	Tamil equivalent using English script
Sit on a chair	oru kathiraiyil iru(nka<u>ll</u>)
Keep it on the table	mehsaiyinmehl vai(yunka<u>ll</u>)
This bed is not comfortable to me	intha kaddil enakku savuhariyamaaha il-lai
Keep the two desks closer	irandu ezhulththu mehsaihalaiyum kidda vai(yunka<u>ll</u>)
Bring that stool here	antha siru naatrkaaliyai inkeh konduvaa (runka<u>ll</u>)

Keep it on the bottom-shelf	athai adiththaddil vai(yunka<u>ll</u>)
Close that door	antha-k-kathavai pooddu(nka<u>ll</u>)
Open the windows	jannalha<u>l</u>lai-th-thira(vunkall)

EXERCISE 15

1. What are the Tamil words for the following?

   (i) keep   (ii) uncomfortable   (iii) close
   (iv) bring   (v) bottom   (vi) closer   (vii) open

2. Write each sentence in the table above in Tamil script and read it aloud.

LESSON 16

Colours

White, Black, Blue, Green, Red, Yellow, Brown, Pink, Violet

English word	Tamil word written using English script	Tamil word written using Tamil script
White	vellai	வெள்ளை
Black	karuppu	கறுப்பு
Blue	neelam	நீலம்
Green	pachchai	பச்சை
Red	sivappu	சிவப்பு
Yellow	manja__ll__	மஞ்சள்
Brown	manh niram	மண் நிறம்
Pink	i__ll__am sivappu	இளம் சிவப்பு
Violet	uuthaa	ஊதா

Say in Tamil the English sentences given in the first column below:

English sentence	Tamil equivalent using English script
I bought a white hat.	naan oru vei__ll__ __ll__ai-th-thoppi vaankinehn.
Black colour is beautiful.	karuppu niram azhakaanathu.
She wore a blue sari	ava neelach-chehlai uduththiyirunthaa.

The garden was all green.	thohddam muzhuvathum pachchaiyaai irunthathu.
He didn't stop the vehicle at the red light.	avar vaahanaththai sivappu 'light'- il nitpaaddavil-lai.
It is a beautiful yellow flower.	athu oru vadivaana manja<u>ll</u> puu (malar).
The brown dog jumped over the fence.	'brown' niramulla naai vehliyin mehl paainthathu.
The pink dress suited her well.	i<u>ll</u>am sivappu niramaana udai avavukku nal-la poruththamaayi irunththathu.
I like violet colour	enakku uuthaa niram viruppam.

EXERCISE 16

1. What are the Tamil words for the following?

   (i) hat   (ii) bought   (iii) colour   (iv) garden
   (v) flower   (vi) dog   (vii) jumped   (viii) fence

2. Write each sentence in the table above in Tamil script and read it aloud.

LESSON 17

Greetings & Salutations

'Good morning', 'Good night', 'How are you?', 'Thank you', 'Thank you very much', 'Happy Birthday', 'Happy Anniversary'.

English word	Tamil equivalent written using English script	Tamil equivalent written using Tamil script
Good morning	kaalai vanakkam	காலை வணக்கம்
Good night	nalliravaahuha	நல்லிரவாகுக
How are you?	eppadi irukkireer(ha<u>ll</u>)	எப்படி இருக்கிறீர்(கள்)
Thank you	nantri / upakaaram	நன்றி / உபகாரம்
Thank you very much	mihavum nantri/ mihapperiya upakaaram	மிகவும் நன்றி / மிகப் பெரிய உபகாரம்
Happy Birthday	pirantha naa<u>ll</u> vaazhthukkal	பிறந்த நாள் வாழ்த்துக்கள்
Happy Anniversary	aandu vizhaa vaazhthukka<u>ll</u>	ஆண்டு விழா வாழ்த்துக்கள்

Say in Tamil the English sentences given in the first column below:

English sentence	Tamil equivalent using English script
Good morning, Sir	kaalai vanakkam, aiyaa
Have a good night	unka<u>ll</u> iravu nal-lirvaahuha
How are you, brother?	eppadi irukkireer sahohtharan?

I say thank you	naan nantri kuurukirehn
I thank you very much for your hospitality	umathu upasarippukku mikka nantri
Wish you a happy birthday	unka<u>ll</u>ukku pirantha naa<u>ll</u> vaazhthukka<u>ll</u>
Wish you happy anniversary	umakku aandu vizhaa vaazhthukka<u>ll</u>
I wish you happy wedding anniversary	umakku-th-thirumanha aandu vizhaa vaazhthukka<u>ll</u>

EXERCISE 17

1. What are the Tamil words for the following?

    (i) sir   (ii) brother   (iii) hospitality
    (iv) wish   (v) wedding

2. Write each sentence in the table above in Tamil script and read it aloud.

LESSON 18

Commands

Come, Go, Bring, Take, Walk, Run, Jump, Stop, Start

English word	Tamil word written using English script	Tamil word written using Tamil script
Come	vaa / vaarunka<u>ll</u>	வா / வாருங்கள்
Go	poh / pohnka<u>ll</u>	போ / போங்கள்
Bring	konduvaa (runka<u>ll</u>)	கொண்டுவா / கொண்டு வாருங்கள்
Take	edu(nka<u>ll</u>)	எடு / எடுங்கள்
Walk	nada / nadavunka<u>ll</u>	நட / நடவுங்கள்
Run	Ohdu / ohdunka<u>ll</u>	ஓடு / ஓடுங்கள்
Jump	kuthi / kuthiyunka<u>ll</u>	குதி / குதியுங்கள்
Stop	nirruththu(nka<u>ll</u>)	நிறுத்து / நிறுத்துங்கள்
Start	aarampi / aarampiyunka<u>ll</u>	ஆரம்பி / ஆரம்பியுங்கள்

Say in Tamil the English sentences given in the first column below:

English sentence	Tamil equivalent using English script
Please come soon	thayavuseythu kethiyaayi vaarunka<u>ll</u>.
You go home	nee veeddukku-p- poh (neenka<u>ll</u> veeddukku-p-pohnka<u>ll</u>)
Take the short route	kurukku vazhiyai edunka<u>ll</u>
Walk fast	viraivaaha nadavunka<u>ll</u>
I am going to run	naan ohdappohhirehn

59

Jump over the fence	vehli mehlaal paayi(unka<u>ll</u>)
Stop here	inkeh nirruththu(nka<u>ll</u>)
Start now	ippa aarampi(yunka<u>ll</u>)

EXERCISE 18

1. What are the Tamil words for the following?

   (i) please   (ii) soon   (iii) home   (iv) short
   (v) route   (vi) fast   (vii) fence   (viii) now

2. Write each sentence in the table above in Tamil script and read it aloud.

3. Match a picture to a word.

(a)   (1) மரம்

(b) 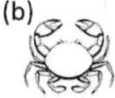   (2) நண்டு

(c)    (3) பந்து

(d)    (4) மீன்

(e)    (5) குரங்கு

LESSON 19
Directions

Straight, Right side, Left side, Up, Down, North, South, East, West

English word	Tamil word written using English script	Tamil word written using Tamil script
Straight	nehr / nehta	நேர் / நேர
Right side	valathu pakkam	வலது பக்கம்
Left side	Idathu pakkam	இடது பக்கம்
Up	mehl / mehleh	மேல் / மேலே
Down	kiizh / kiizheh	கீழ் / கீழே
North	vadakku	வடக்கு
South	thetrku	தெற்கு
East	kizhakku	கிழக்கு
West	mehtrku	மேற்கு

Say in Tamil the English sentences given in the first column below:

English sentence	Tamil equivalent using English script
Go straight	nehra poh(nkall).
Turn right	valappakkam thitumpu(nkall)
Turn left	idappakkam thitumpu(nkall)
Go up	mehleh poh(nkall)
Go down	kiizheh poh(nkall)

We live in the South side	naanka<u>ll</u> thetrku-p-pakkaththil vasikkirohm
Jaffna is in the North of Sri Lanka	Yaalpaanam Ilankaiyin vadappakkaththil irukkirathu
Sun rises in the East	sooriyan kizhakkil uthikkirathu
Sun sets in the West	sooriyan mehtrkil maraihirathu

EXERCISE 19

1. What are the Tamil words for the following?

    (i) go (ii) turn (iii) live (iv) side
    (v) sun (vi) rises (vii) sets

2. Write each sentence in the table above in Tamil script and read it aloud.

LESSON 20

Relatives (1)

Father, Mother, Son, Daughter, Older sister, Younger sister, Older brother, Younger brother.

English word	Tamil word written using English script	Tamil word written using Tamil script
Father	thahappan/appa/aiyaa	தகப்பன்/அப்பா/ஐயா
Mother	thaayi/amma	தாய்/அம்மா
Son	mahan	மகன்
Daughter	maha<u>ll</u>	மகள்
Older sister	muuththa sahohthari/ akka	மூத்த சகோதரி/அக்கா
Younger sister	izhaiya sahohthari / thankai	இழைய சகோதரி / தங்கை
Older brother	muuththa sahohtharan / annan	மூத்த சகோதரன் / அண்ணன்
Younger brother	izhaiya sahohtharan / thambi	இழைய சகோதரன் / தம்பி

Say in Tamil the English sentences given in the first column below:

English sentence	Tamil equivalent using English script
What is your father's occupation?	unka<u>ll</u>udaiya thahappanin(appaavin) uththiyohkam enna?
Where is your mother?	unka<u>ll</u>udaiya thaayi(ammaah) enkeh?
Is this your son?	ivar unka<u>ll</u>udaiya mahanaa?
How many daughters have you?	unka<u>ll</u>ukku eththanai maha<u>ll</u>maar?
How old is your older sister?	unka<u>ll</u>udaiya akkavukku eththanai vayathu?
What is your younger sister doing?	unka<u>ll</u>udaiya thankai enna seihiraa?
Is he your older brother?	avar unka<u>ll</u>udaiya annanaa?
How many younger brothers do you have?	unka<u>ll</u>ukku eththanai thampiha<u>ll</u>?

EXERCISE 20

1. What are the Tamil words for the following?

    (i) occupation (ii) how many (iii) older (iv) younger

2. Write each sentence in the table above in Tamil script and read it aloud.

LESSON 21

Relatives (2)

Uncle, Aunt, Sister-in-law, Brother-in-law, Grandfather, Grandmother

English word	Tamil word written using English script	Tamil word written using Tamil script
Uncle	maamaa	மாமா
Aunt	maami	மாமி
Sister-in-law	maiththunhi	மைத்துணி
Brother-in-law	maiththunhan	மைத்துணன்
Grand father	thaaththaa	தாத்தா
Grand mother	paaddi	பாட்டி

குடும்பம்
(Family)

Say in Tamil the English sentences given in the first column below:

English sentence	Tamil equivalent using English script
Who is your uncle?	yaar unka<u>l</u>ludaiya maamaa?
Where does your aunt live?	unka<u>l</u>ludaiya maami enkeh vasikkiraa?
Where does your sister-in-law work?	unka<u>l</u>ludaiya maiththunhi enkeh vehlai seyhiraa?
Your brother-in-law seems to be a nice person	unkalludaiya maiththunhan oru nallavar pohl therihiraar
Is your grandfather here?	unka<u>l</u>ludaiya thaaththaa inkeh irukkiraaraa?
Does your grandmother live with you?	unka<u>l</u>ludaiya paaddi ummudanaa vasikkiraa?

EXERCISE 21

1. What are the Tamil words for the following?

    (i) work   (ii) here   (iii) nice   (iv) live

2. Write each sentence in the table above in Tamil script and read it aloud.

LESSON 22

Relatives (3)

Husband, Wife, Family, Father-in-law, Mother-in-law, Granddaughter, Grand son

English word	Tamil word written using English script	Tamil word written using Tamil script
Husband	kanavan (purusan)	கணவன் / புருசன்
Wife	manaivi (pehnchaathi)	மனைவி / பெண்சாதி
Family	kudumpam	குடும்பம்
Farther in law	maamanaar	மாமனார்
Mother-in-law	maamiyaar	மாமியார்
Grand daughter	pehththi	பேத்தி
Grand son	pehran	பேரன்

Say in Tamil the English sentences given in the first column below:

English sentence	Tamil Pronunciation using English script
Rama is her husband	'Rama' avavudaiya purusan
Balan came with his wife	"Balan' thannudaiya manaiviyudan vanthaar
They are a united family.	avarha<u>ll</u> oru ottrumaiyaana kudumpam
His father-in-law lives here.	avarudaiya maamanaar inku vasikiraar
Her mother-in-law died last year.	avavudaiya maamiyaar pohna varusam iranthupohnaa
Sinnarasa has two beautiful granddaughters.	Sinnarasaavuku vadivaana irandu pehththimaar irukkiraarha<u>ll</u>
Ramesh loves his grandson a lot.	Ramesh-iku- avar pehranil athika anpu.

EXERCISE 22

1. What are the Tamil words for the following?

   (i) came   (ii) united   (iii) died
   (iv) beautiful   (v) loves   (vi) lot

2. Write each sentence in the table above in Tamil script and read it aloud.

LESSON 23

At The Post Office

Post office, Letter, Parcel, Stamp, Envelope, Address

English word	Tamil word written using English script	Tamil word written using Tamil script
Post Office	thapaal ka<u>n</u>thohr	தபால் கந்தோர்
Letter	kaditham	கடிதம்
Parcel	Pottalam	பொட்டலம்
Stamp	muththirai	முத்திரை
Envelope	kaditha urai	கடித உறை
Address	muhavari / vilaasam	முகவரி / விலாசம்

Say in Tamil the English sentences given in the first column below:

English sentence	Tamil Pronunciation using English script
I am going to the post office	naan thapaal kanthohrukku-p-pohhirehn
I need to write another letter	naan innoru kaditham avasiyam ezhutha vehnum.
Please could you post this parcel?	thayavu seythu intha paarsalai-post pannuveera?
Please give me three Rs.50 stamps	thayavu seythu enakku muuntru ayimpathu ruupaa muththiraiha__ll__ thaarunka__ll__
Please give me stamps for a registered letter.	thayavu seythu oru 'registered' kadithaththukku muththiraiha__ll__ thaarunka__ll__.
I will write the postal address on the envelope	naan muhavariyai kaditha uraiyil ezhuthuvehn.

> **EXERCISE 23**
>
> 1. What are the Tamil words for the following?
>
>   (i) going   (ii) another   (iii) need
>   (iv) give   (v) will-write
>
> 2. Write each sentence in the table above in Tamil script and read it aloud.

LESSON 24

Around The House/Hotel

Inside, Outside, Between, Beyond, Upstairs, Downstairs

English word	Tamil word written using English script	Tamil word written using Tamil script
Inside	u<u>ll ll</u>eh	உள்ளே
Outside	ve<u>ll</u>iyeh	வெளியே
Between	idaiyeh	இடையே
Beyond	appaaleh	அப்பாலே
Upstairs	mehl maadi	மேல் மாடி
Downstairs	kiizh maadi	கீழ் மாடி

Say in Tamil, the English sentences given in the first column below:

English sentence	Tamil equivalent using English script
Go inside	ull lleh poh(nkall)
Come outside	velliyeh vaa(runkall)
You are caught in between	neenkall idaiyeh ahappaddu - viddeerhall.
It is beyond the gate	athu kathavukku appaaleh
Go and have a look downstairs	kiizh maadiyil pohyi paar(unkall)
I am going upstairs	naan mehl maadikku pohhirehn
We have to go downstairs	naankall kiizh maadikku pohhavehnum

EXERCISE 24

1. What are the Tamil words for the following?

    (i) caught   (ii) beyond   (iii) look   (iv) going

2. Write each sentence in the table above in Tamil script and read it aloud.

LESSON 25

Counting (1)

One, Two, Three, Four, Five, Six, Seven, Eight, Nine, Ten

English word	Tamil word written using English script	Tamil word written using Tamil script
One	ondu (onru)	ஒண்டு (ஒன்று)
Two	irandu	இரண்டு
Three	muundu (muunru)	மூண்டு (மூன்று)
Four	naalu	நாலு
Five	ainchu (ainthu)	ஐஞ்சு (ஐந்து)
Six	aaru	ஆறு
Seven	ehzhu	ஏழு
Eight	eddu	எட்டு
Nine	onpathu	ஒன்பது
Ten	paththu	பத்து

Say in Tamil the English sentences given in the first column below:

English sentence	Tamil Pronunciation using English script
One country one nation	oru naadu oru thehsam

The two hearts are united	iru ithayanka<u>ll</u> inhainthana
A square has four corners	oru sathuraththukku naalu muulaiha<u>ll</u>
Five medals were won by Mohan	'Mohan' ainthu pathakkanka<u>ll</u>ai venraar
There are six sides for a die	oru thaaya-k-kaddaikku aaru pakkanka<u>ll</u>
Is Seven a lucky number?	ehzhu oru athirsda ilakkamaa?
Eight churches are in this city	intha nakaraththil eddu kohvilha<u>ll</u> irukkinrana
Nine planets affect the humans	onpathu kirahanka<u>ll</u> manitharai thaakkuhinrana
Follow the ten commandments of God	kadavu<u>ll</u>in paththu katrpanaiha<u>ll</u>ai anusarikkavum

EXERCISE 25

1. What are the Tamil words for the following?

   (i) nation   (ii) heart   (iii) corner
   (iv) medals   (v) side   (vi) lucky-number
   (vii) church   (viii) planet   (ix) commandments

2. Write each sentence in the table above in Tamil script and read it aloud.

LESSON 26

Counting (2)

Eleven, Twelve, Thirteen, Fourteen, Fifteen, Sixteen, Seventeen, Eighteen, Nineteen, Twenty

English word	Tamil word written using English script	Tamil word written using Tamil script
Eleven	pathinonhdu	பதினொண்டு
Twelve	pantendu (pannirendu)	பன்ரெண்டு
Thirteen	pathinmuundu	பதின் மூண்டு
Fourteen	pathinaalu	பதி நாலு
Fifteen	pathinainthu	பதினைந்து
Sixteen	pathinaaru	பதினாறு
Seventeen	pathinehzhu	பதினேழு
Eighteen	pathineddu	பதினெட்டு
Nineteen	paththonpathu	பத்தொன்பது
Twenty	irupathu	இருபது

Say in Tamil the English sentences given in the first column below:

English sentence	Tamil Pronunciation using English script
Ten plus one is eleven	paththum ondum pathinondu
Fifteen less five is ten	pathinainthil ainthu kurainththaal paththu
Twelve is less than fourteen	pantendu pathinaalilum siriyathu
Sixteen is greater than thirteen	pathinaaru pathinmuundilum periyathu
Seventeen is an odd number	pathinehzhu oru ottrai ilakkam
Ten is an even number	paththu oru iraddai ilakkam
Twelve items mean a dozen items	pannirandu sarakkuka_ll_ oru 'dozen' enappadum

EXERCISE 26

1. What are the Tamil words for the following?

    (i) less   (ii) greater   (iii) odd   (iv) even

2. Write each sentence in the table above in Tamil script and read it aloud.

LESSON 27

Counting (3)

Ten, Twenty, Thirty, Forty, Fifty, Sixty, Seventy, Eighty, Ninety, One hundred.

English word	Tamil word written using English script	Tamil word written using Tamil script
Ten	paththu	பத்து
Twenty	irupathu	இருபது
Thirty	muppathu	முப்பது
Forty	naatpathu	நாற்பது
Fifty	ayimpathu	ஐம்பது
Sixty	arupathu	அறுபது
Seventy	ezhupathu	எழுபது
Eighty	ehnpathu	எண்பது
Ninety	thohnnhuuru	தொண்ணூறு
One hundred	nuuru	நூறு

Say in Tamil the English sentences given in the first column below:

English sentence	Tamil Pronunciation using English script
Ten and ten makes twenty	paththum paththum itupathu.
Two times twenty is forty	irandu tharam irupathu naatrpathu.
Eighty less thirty is fifty	enhpathil irunthu muppathu pohnaal ayimpathu.
Five goes into hundred twenty times	Ainthu, nuurukku<u>ll</u> irupathu tharam pohkum.
One hundred means a century	nuuru enraal oru 'century'.
How much is thirty-six and forty-two?	muppaththi aarum naatrpaththi irandum evvalavu?
Not seven times seven but seven times seventy	ehzhu tharam ehzhu alla, aanaal ehzhu tharam ezhupathu.

> **EXERCISE 27**
>
> 1. What are the Tamil words for the following?
>
>   (i) times   (ii) means   (iii) century   (iv) but
>
> 2. Write each sentence in the table above in Tamil script and read it aloud.

LESSON 28

Counting (4)

Learn to count from:

21 – 30; 31 – 40; 41 – 50; 51 – 60;
61 – 70; 71 – 80; 81 – 90; 91 – 100

The counting is similar to that from 11 – 20. Only the prefixes change as follows:

Twenty is **irupathu**

Numbers from 21 – 29, the prefix is "**irupaththi**".

That is,
 irupaththi-ondu, irupaththi-irandu and so on.

Thirty is **muppathu**

Numbers from 31 – 39, the prefix is "**muppaththi**".

That is,
 muppaththi-ondu, muppaththi- irandu and so on.

Forty is **naatpathu**

Numbers from 41 – 49, the prefix is "**naatpaththi**".

That is,
 naatpaththi-ondu, naatpaththi-irandu and so on.

Fifty is **aimpathu**

Numbers from 51 – 59, the prefix is "**aimpaththi**".

That is,
 aimpaththi-ondu, aimpaththi-irandu and so on.

Sixty is **arupathu**

Numbers from 61 – 69, the prefix is "**arupaththi**".

That is,
    arupaththi-ondu, arupaththi-irandu and so on.

Seventy is **ezhupathu**

Numbers from 71 – 79, the prefix is "**ezhupaththi**".

That is,
    ezhupaththi-ondu, ezhupaththi-irandu and so on.

Eighty is **enhpathu**

Numbers from 81 – 89, the prefix is "**enhpaththi**".

That is,
    enhpaththi-ondu, enhpaththi-irandu and so on.

Ninety is **thonhnhuuru**

Numbers from 91 – 99, the prefix is "**thonhnhuutri**".

That is,
    thonhnhuutri-ondu, thonhnhuutri-irandu and so on.

One Hundred is **nuuru**

EXERCISE 28

Practise counting from 1 to 100 in Tamil, ten times.

LESSON 29

Counting (5)

One hundred, Two hundred, Three hundred, Four hundred, Five hundred, Six hundred, Seven hundred, Eight hundred, Nine hundred, One thousand

English word	Tamil word written using English script	Tamil word written using Tamil script
One hundred	nuuru	நூறு
Two hundred	irunuuru	இருநூறு
Three hundred	munnuuru	முந்நூறு
Four hundred	naanuuru	நாநூறு
Five hundred	ainuuru	ஐநூறு
Six hundred	arunuuru	அறுநூறு
Seven hundred	ezhunuuru	எழுநூறு
Eight hundred	ehnnhuuru	எண்ணூறு
Nine hundred	thozhaayiram	தொழாயிரம்
One thousand	aayirum	ஆயிரம்

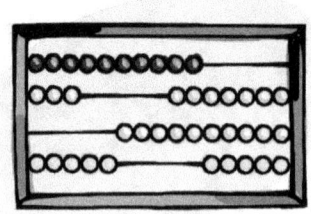

Say in Tamil the English sentences given in the first column below:

English sentence	Tamil Pronunciation using English script
One hundred and fifty percent	nuutri aimpathu veetham.
Two hundred and twenty runs	irunuutri irupathu ohddanka<u>ll</u>.
Two hundred years' old	irunuuru varudankall palaiyana
Four hundred years ago	naanuuru varudanka<u>ll</u>ukku munpu
There are six hundred students	arunuuru maanavarha<u>ll</u> irukkiraarha<u>ll</u>
Seven hundred entrance tickets were sold	ezhunuuru nuzhaivu-ch-cheedduha<u>ll</u> vilaippaddana
The collection came up to nearly one thousand dollars	vasool kiddaththadda aayiram 'dollars' maddil vanthathu
We are talking in thousands	naanka<u>ll</u> aayiraththil kathaikkirohm

> **EXERCISE 29**
>
> 1. What are the Tamil words for the following?
>
>   (i) percent (ii) runs (iii) old (iv) ago (v) students
>   (vi) sold (vii) collection (viii) nearly (ix) talking
>
> 2. Write each sentence in the table above in Tamil script and read it aloud.

LESSON 30

Counting (6)

Ten thousand, Twenty thousand, Thirty thousand, Forty thousand, Fifty thousand, Sixty thousand, Seventy thousand, Eighty thousand, Ninety thousand, One hundred thousand.

English word	Tamil word written using English script	Tamil word written using Tamil script
Ten thousand	paththaayiram	பத்தாயிரம்
Twenty thousand	irupathaayiram	இருபதாயிரம்
Thirty thousand	muppathaayiram	முப்பதாயிரம்
Forty thousand	naatpathaayiram	நாற்பதாயிரம்
Fifty thousand	ayimpathaayiram	ஐம்பதாயிரம்
Sixty thousand	arupathaayiram	அறுபதாயிரம்
Seventy thousand	ezhupathaayiram	எழுபதாயிரம்
Eighty thousand	enhpathaayiram	எண்பதாயிரம்
Ninety thousand	thonhnhuuraayiram	தொண்ணூறாயிரம்
One hundred thousand (one Lakh)	nuuraayiram (Oru iladcham)	நூறாயிரம் (ஒரு இலட்சம்)

Say in Tamil the English sentences given in the first column below:

English sentence	Tamil Pronunciation using English script
One hundred thousand is called a lakh	nuuraayiraththai oru ladcham endu kuuruvohm
Ten lakhs make a million	paththu ladcham oru 'million'
A thousand million is called a billion	aayiram 'million' ai oru 'billion' endu kuuruvohm
A million million is a trillion	oru 'million' 'million' ai oru 'trillion' endu kuuruvohm
There are more than 26 million people in Sri Lanka	Ilankaiyil 26 'million' makkalukkumehl irukkiraarka<u>ll</u>
Hundreds of thousand Sri Lankans have gone to live in other countries	nuuraayirak kanakkaana Ilankaiyar vehru naaduka<u>ll</u>ukku vasikka pohyividdaarha<u>ll</u>
There are many millionaires in Sri Lanka	Ilankaiyil pala 'millionaires' irukkiraarha<u>ll</u>

> **EXERCISE 30**
>
> 1. What are the Tamil words for the following?
>
>   (i) many   (ii) more   (iii) live   (iv) countries
>
> 2. Write six numbers (of your choice) between 500,000 and 600 000 and say them aloud in Tamil.

LESSON 31

Place Counting

First, Second, Third, Fourth, Fifth, Sixth, Seventh, Eighth, Ninth, Tenth etc.

English word	Tamil word written using English script	Tamil word written using Tamil script
First	muthalaavathu	முதலாவது
Second	irandaavathu	இரண்டாவது
Third	muunraavathu	மூன்றாவது
Fourth	naalaavathu	நாலாவது
Fifth	ayinthaavathu	ஐந்தாவது
Sixth	aaraavathu	ஆறாவது
Seventh	ehzhaavathu	ஏழாவது
Eighth	eddaavathu	எட்டாவது
Ninth	onpathaavathu	ஒன்பதாவது
Tenth	paththaavathu	பத்தாவது

Say in Tamil the English sentences given in the first column below:

English sentence	Tamil equivalent using English script
Out of the five children first three are males.	ayinthu pill llaikallil muthal muunrum aanhkall

I am the fourth born in the family	enathu kudumpaththil naan naalaavathaaha piranthehn
Siva was the fifth one to arrive	'Siva' ainthaavathaaha varukai thanthaar
Third place receives bronze medal	muunraavathu idaththukku venhkala pathakkam kidaikkirathu
Sundar came second in the race	'Sundar' ohddapppanthayaththil irandaavathaaka vanthaar
He came first in the class	avar vahuppil muthalaavathaaha vanthaar
What is the seventh item in the agenda?	seyal thiddaththil ehzhaavathaaha enna irukkirathu

EXERCISE 31

1. What are the Tamil words for the following?

   (i) children   (ii) born   (iii) family   (iv) arrive
   (v) receives   (vi) race   (vii) agenda

2. Write each sentence in the table above in Tamil script and read it aloud.

LESSON 32

Telling The Time

Nine, Nine fifteen, Nine thirty, Nine forty-five, One twenty, Twelve, Two twenty-five, Ten to six, Twenty past eight, Eleven fifty, Quarter to ten, Half past five.

English word	Tamil word written using English script	Tamil word written using Tamil script
Nine o'clock	onpathu manhi	ஒன்பது மணி
Nine fifteen	onpathu pathinayinchu	ஒன்பது பதினைஞ்சு
Nine thirty	onpathu muppathu	ஒன்பது முப்பது
Nine forty-five	onpathu naatpaththayinchu	ஒன்பது நாற்பத்தைஞ்சு
One twenty	ondu irupathu	ஒண்டு இருபது
Twelve	pannirandu	பன்னிரண்டு
Two twenty-five	irandu irupaththiayinchu	இரண்டு இருபத்தைஞ்சு
Ten to six	Aarukku-p-paththu nimidam	ஆறுக்கு பத்து நிமிடம்
Twenty past eight	eddu irupathu	எட்டு இருபது
Eleven fifty	pathinondu aimpathu	பதினொண்டு ஐம்பது
Quarter to ten	onpatheh mukkaal	ஒன்பதே முக்கால்
Half past five	aintharai	ஐந்தரை

Say in Tamil the English sentences given in the first column below:

English sentence	Tamil equivalent using English script
What is the time now?	ippa nehram enna?
What time does the show start	eththanai manikku kaadchi thodankukirathu?
What time is he coming?	avar eththanai manikku vaaraar?
She always keeps to time	ava eppavum nehraththai kadaipidippaa
The match will start at half past seven	pohddi ehzharaikku aarampikkum
It is better to go half an hour early	arai maniththiyaalam ve_ll_ _ll_ena pohvathu nal-lathu
My watch is running fifteen minutes fast	ennudaiya kadihaaram pathinainthu nimidam munthi ohduthu.

EXERCISE 32

1. What are the Tamil words for the following?

   (i) now (ii) show (iii) start (iv) coming
   (v) always (vi) match (vii) better (viii) early
   (ix) watch (x) fast

2. Read aloud the following :

   ஆங்கில ஜனவரி மாதத்தை தமிழில் 'தை மாதம்' எனக் கூறுவர். தமிழுக்கு என்று ஒரு தனி கலண்டர் உண்டு. தமிழ் தை முதல் நாள் ஆங்கில மாதம் ஜனவரி 14ஆம் அல்லது 15ஆம் திகதிக்கு சமம். தை முதல் நாளில் பொங்கல் விழாவைக் கொண்டாடுவர். இதனால் பொங்கல் விழா, தைப் பொங்கல் விழா என்று அழைக்கப்படுகிறது.

LESSON 33

Common Words

No, Yes, Certain, Correct, Nothing, Everything, Something.

English word	Tamil word written using English script	Tamil word written using Tamil script
No	illai	இல்லை
Yes	aam/ohm	ஆம் / ஓம்
Certain	nichchayam / kaddaayam	நிச்சயம் / கட்டாயம்
Correct	sariyaana	சரியான
Nothing	ondumil-lai	ஒன்டுமில்லை
Everything	el-laam / el-laththaiyum	எல்லாம் / எல்லாத்தையும்
Something	ehthaavathu / ehtoh	ஏதாவது / ஏதோ

Say in Tamil the English sentences given in the first column below:

English sentence	Tamil equivalent using English script
No, I am not going today	illai, naan inhdaikku pohhavillai
Yes, I will be meeting him tomorrow	ohm, naan avarai naalaikku santhippehn
I am pretty certain about that	athaipatty naan nichchayamaha solvehn

There is no correct answer for that	athatrku sariyaana marumozhi illai
I have nothing to hide	naan marraippathatrku ondumillai
He gives careful thought to everything	avar el-laththaiyum kavanamaaka yohsanai seyvaar
There is something wrong with him	avaril ehtoh pizhai irukkuthu

EXERCISE 33

1. What are the Tamil words for the following?

    (i) today   (ii) meeting   (iii) tomorrow
    (iv) answer   (v) hide   (vi) careful
    (vii) thought   (viii) wrong.

2. Read aloud the following Passage:

மொத்தமாக 1330 குறள்களை தந்து அதன் மூலம் மக்களுக்கு நன்னெறிகளை உணர்த்தியவர் தான் திருவள்ளுவர். மக்கள் தங்கள் வாழ்க்கையில் எவ்வாறு நடந்துகொள்ளவேண்டும் என்பதனை தனது 133 அதிகாரங்கள் மூலம் தெளிவாக பல நூறு வருடங்களுக்கு முன்னரே இந்த உலகிற்கு தெரிவித்து சென்றவர் என்ற பெருமை திருவள்ளுவருக்கு உண்டு. ஒவ்வொரு குறளும் (couplets) இரண்டு வரிகள்தான் கொண்டவை. உதாரணமாக முதல் குறள்:

அகர முதல எழுத்தெல்லாம்
ஆதி பகவன் முதற்றே உலகு

The meaning in English is: 'அ' is the prime of all Tamil letters. Similarly, God is the prime of the world.

LESSON 34

Months Of the Year

January, February, March, April, May, June, July, August, September, October, November, December

English word	Tamil word written using English script	Tamil word written using Tamil script
January	thai	தை
February	maasi	மாசி
March	pankuni	பங்குனி
April	siththirai	சித்திரை
May	vaihaasi	வைகாசி
June	aani	ஆனி
July	aadi	ஆடி
August	aavanhi	ஆவணி
September	puraddaasi	புரட்டாசி
October	aippasi	ஐப்பசி
November	kaarththikai	கார்த்திகை
December	maarkazhi	மார்கழி

Say in Tamil the English sentences given in the first column below:

English sentence	Tamil Equivalent using English script
It rains here in January	inku thaiyil mazhai peyyum

February and March are busy months for me	enakku maasiyum pankuniyum surusuruppaana maathanka_ll_
I am going overseas in April	naan siththiraiyil ve_ll_inaadu pohhirehn
My birthday falls in the month of May	enathu pirantha naa_ll_ vaihasi maathaththil varukirathu
June is the end of financial year for us	enka_ll_ukku 'financial' varuda mudivu aaniyil
July, August, and September will be very cold here	aadi, aavanhi, puraddaasiyil inku nalla ku_ll_ir
Christmas seems to start in October	'Christmas' aippasiyil thodankuvathu pohl thetikirathu
My mother in law's death anniversary comes in November	enathu maamiyaarin irantha aandu ninaivu thinam kaarthihaiyil varum
The school holidays start here around mid-December	paadasaalai vidumurai inku maarkazhi naduvil aarampikkum

EXERCISE 34

1. Write the Tamil words for the following and read them aloud.

   (i) rains   (ii) busy   (iii) overseas
   (iv) birthday (v) cold   (vi) anniversary

2. Translate the following into Tamil:

   The school holidays for Christmas start here around last week of November.

LESSON 35
Days Of the Week

Sunday, Monday, Tuesday, Wednesday, Thursday, Friday, Saturday

English word	Tamil word written using English script	Tamil word written using Tamil script
Sunday	gnaayiru	ஞாயிறு
Monday	thinka__ll__	திங்கள்
Tuesday	sevvaayi	செவ்வாய்
Wednesday	puthan	புதன்
Thursday	viyaazhan	வியாழன்
Friday	ve__ll__ __ll__i	வெள்ளி
Saturday	sani	சனி

Say in Tamil the English sentences given in the first column below:

English sentence	Tamil Equivalent using English script
Sunday is a holiday for most people	palarukku gnaayiru oru vidumurai
I have to meet someone early on Monday morning	naan oruvarai thinka__ll__ athi - kaalaiyil santhikka vehnum
I want to watch the cricket match on Tuesday	naan sevvaayi kizhamai 'cricket' pohddi paarkka vehnum

My flight is on Wednesday night	enathu vimaana -p- payanam puthan iravu
Shall we go to a restaurant for lunch on Thursday?	naanka<u>ll</u> viyaazhan mathiya saapaaddukku oru 'restraurant' ikku pohvohmaa?
We can have the party on next Friday night	naaankall 'party' ai aduththa ve<u>ll</u> <u>ll</u>i iravu vaikkalaam
I am getting some visitors on Saturday	sani-k- kizhamai ennidam sila virunththaathiha<u>ll</u> varuhiraarha<u>ll</u>

EXERCISE 35

1. Write the Tamil words for the following and read them aloud.

   (i) holiday (ii) someone (iii) night (iv) flight
   (v) lunch (vi) next (vii) visitors

2. Read aloud the following Passage:

   கிறிஸ்தவக் கொண்டாட்டங்களுக்கு ஒதுக்கப்பட்ட அரசு விடுமுறை நாள்கள் **பெரிய_வெள்ளி** (Good Friday), மற்றும் கிறிஸ்து பிறப்புப் பெருவிழா நாள் (Christmas Day) மார்கழி 25ஆம் நாள் ஆகும். கிறிஸ்தவர்கள் ஆலயங்களுக்குச் சென்று வழிபாடு நடத்துவர். கத்தோலிக்கர் திருப்பலியில் கலந்துகொண்டு நற்கருணை விருந்தில் பங்கேற்பர்.

   கிறிஸ்தவர்களோடு பிற சமயத்தவரும் இணைந்து இவ்விழாவைக் கொண்டாடுகின்றனர். இது சமய நல்லிணக்கம் உருவாக உறுதுணையாக உள்ளது என்பதில் ஐயமில்லை.

LESSON 36

Workers

Teacher, Priest, Engineer, Doctor, Lawyer, Nurse, Clerk, Accountant, Policeman

English word	Tamil word written using English script	Tamil word written using Tamil script
Teacher	vaaththiyaar / aasiriyar	வாத்தியார் / ஆசிரியர்
Priest	archchahar / kuruvaanavar / puusaari	அர்ச்சகர் / குருவானவர்/ பூசாரி
Engineer	porriyiyalaalar	பொறியியலாளர்
Doctor	vaiththiyar	வைத்தியர்
Lawyer	vazhakkarignar / saddaththaranhi	வழக்கறிஞர் / சட்டத்தரணி
Nurse	thaathi	தாதி
Clerk	kumaasthaa	குமாஸ்தா
Accountant	kanhakkaalar	கணக்காளர்
Policeman	poliskaaran	பொலிஸ்காரன்

Note: A new borrowed alphabet 'ஸ்' with the sound "is" has been introduced in this lesson.

Say in Tamil the English sentences given in the first column below:

English sentence	Tamil Equivalent using English script
He is a good teacher	avar oru nal-la aasiriyar

I have to see a priest	naan oru archchakarai kaanhavehnhum
Ramana works as an engineer	'Ramana' oru poriyiyalaalaraaka vehlai seyhiraar
I have an appointment with the doctor	enakku vaiththiyarudan oru sa<u>n</u>thippu munpathivu ('appointment') irukkuthu
I will have to consult my lawyer	naan oru vazhakkarignarudan aalohsikka vehnhum
Mala is the head nurse at the hospital	'Mala' aaspaththiriyil thalaimai –th-thaathi
John is just a clerk	'John' oru verum kumaasthaa
Suresan is a brilliant accountant	'Suresan' oru sirappu vaayi<u>n</u>tha kanakkaalar
Police arrested Gopi yesterday	'Gopi'ai poliskaarar nehtru kaithu seythaarhall

EXERCISE 36

1. Write the Tamil words for the following and read them aloud.

   (i) works   (ii) appointment   (iii) consult
   (iv) hospital   (v) brilliant   (vi) yesterday

2. Write each sentence in the table above in Tamil script and read it aloud.

LESSON 37

Evils

War, Fight, Enemy, Murder, Kill, Assassinate

English word	Tamil word written using English script	Tamil word written using Tamil script
War	yuththam / pohr	யுத்தம் / போர்
Fight	sandai	சண்டை
Enemy	ethiri	எதிரி
Murder	kolai	கொலை
Kill	saakadi / kol	சாகடி / கொல்
Assassinate	thiddam theeddik kol	திட்டம் திட்டிக் கொல்

யுத்தம் நிறுத்தப்பட வேணும்!

The war needs to be stopped!

Say in Tamil the English sentences given in the first column below:

English sentence	Tamil equivalent using English script
The war needs to stop	yuththam niruthappada vehnum
We must fight for freedom	naankal suthanthiraththitkaaha sandai pohduvohm
He is not my enemy	avan ennudaiya ethiri alla
He was arrested for murder	avan kolaikkaaha kaithu seyya paddaan
Kill that poisonous snake	antha visappaampai kol-lavum
There was a plan to assassinate the President	Janaathipathiayi kol-la oru thiddam irunthathu

---

EXERCISE 37

1. Write the Tamil words for the following and read them aloud.

    (i) stop   (ii) freedom   (iii) poisonous
    (iv) snake   (v) plan   (vi) president

2. Search 'YouTube' and listen to the nursery rhyme:

    கைவீசம்மா கைவீசு......
    Kai Veesamma kaiveesu...

LESSON 38

Creatures (1)

Dog, Cat, Crow, Hen, Cock, Fly, Mosquito, Grasshopper, Rat, Squirrel.

English word	Tamil word written using English script	Tamil word written using Tamil script
Dog	naai	நாய்
Cat	puunai	பூனை
Crow	kaaham	காகம்
Hen	kohzhi	கோழி
Cock	sehval	சேவல்
Fly	iiy	ஈ
Mosquito	nu<u>l</u>lampu	நுளம்பு / கொசு
Grasshopper	thaththuveddi	தத்துவெட்டி
Rat	eli	எலி
Squirrel	anhil	அணில்

Say in Tamil the English sentences given in the first column below:

English sentence	Tamil Equivalent using English script
I had a dog as a pet for a long time	naan chellamaaha oru naaiyai pala kaalam vaithirunthehn

My wife adores cats.	ennudaiya manaivikku puunaiha__ll__il mihavum nehsam
I don't see many crows these days	intha naadka__ll__il naan pala kaahankallai kaanhpathil-lai
Our hens laid lot of eggs	emathu kozhiha__ll__ kanakka muddaiha__ll__ iddana
I heard the cock crow this morning	naan indaikku kaalaiyil sehval kuuvak kehddehn
Could you please kill that fly?	thayavu seythu antha eeyai kol-luveerhalaa?
Don't forget to apply the mosquito cream	nulampu 'cream' pohda marrakka vehndaam
I haven't seen a grasshopper for a long time	pala kaalamaaha naan thaththuveddi onrai kaanavil-lai
I was enjoying the cat torturing the rat	naan puunai eliyai siththiravathai seyvathai rasiththehn
My son's favourite pet in Sri Lanka was the squirrel	ilankaiyil enathu mahanin mihappiriyamaana sellappiraani anhil

EXERCISE 38

1. Write the Tamil words for the following and read them aloud.

    (i) long time (ii) adore   (iii) laid   (iv) eggs
    (v) lot   (vi) please (vii) apply
    (viii) torturing (ix) pet   (x) favourite

2. Search 'YouTube' and listen to the nursery rhyme:

    "நிலா நிலா ஓடிவா………."
    (Nila Nila Ohdivaa)

LESSON 39

Creatures (2)

Cow, Bull, Goat, Pig, Fox, Rabbit, Deer, Lion, Elephant, Tiger

English word	Tamil word written using English script	Tamil word written using Tamil script
Cow	pasu / maadu	பசு / மாடு
Bull	eruthu	எருது
Goat	aadu	ஆடு
Pig	panhdi (panri)	பண்டி (பன்றி)
Fox	nati	நரி
Rabbit	muyal	முயல்
Deer	maan	மான்
Lion	sinkam	சிங்கம்
Elephant	yaanai	யானை
Tiger	puli	புலி

Say in Tamil the English sentences given in the first column below:

English sentence	Tamil Equivalent using English script
My mother used to milk the cow every morning	ennudaiya ammah ovvoru kaalamaiyilum maaddilai paal karrappaa

Bulls pull carts	eruthuha_ll_ vanhdilha_ll_ai izhukkum
Goat meat curry is quite tasty	aaddu irraichchi karri nalla urusai
Pig is a filthy animal	panhdi oru uuththai miruham
You can see foxes on this road	intha theruvil narihalai paarkalaam
I have a rabbit in my house	naan ennudaiya veeddilai oru muyal vaiththirukkirehn
You could find deer in this forest	intha kaaddilai maanka_ll_ai kaanha mudiyum
Shall we go to see the elephants bathe?	naanka_ll_ yaanaiha_ll_ ku_ll_ippathai paarka pohvamaa?
Tigers and lions can be seen in the Zoo	miruhakkaadchi chaalaiyil puliha_ll_aiyum singanka_ll_aiyum paarka mudiyum

EXERCISE 39

1. Write the Tamil words for the following and read them aloud.

   (i) mother   (ii) every   (iii) cart   (iv) pull   (v) tasty
   (vi) filthy   (vii) road   (viii) house   (ix) forest   (x) bathe
   (xi) zoo

2. Read aloud the following:

   வேண்டுதல் வேண்டாமை இலானடி சேர்ந்தார்க்கு
   யாண்டும் இடும்பை இல.

   அதாவது:
   விருப்பு வெறுப்பு இல்லாத கடவுளின் திருவடிகளை
   பொருந்தி நினைக்கின்றவர்க்கு எப்போதும் எவ்விடத்திலும்
   துன்பம் இல்லை.

LESSON 40

Creatures (3)

Tortoise, Turtle, Spider, Snail, Leach, Frog, Lizard, Centipede, Snake

English word	Tamil word written using English script	Tamil word written using Tamil script
Tortoise/Turtle	aamai	ஆமை
Spider	chilanthi	சிலந்தி
Snail	naththai	நத்தை
Leech	addai	அட்டை
Frog	thavakkai	தவக்கை
Lizard	palli	பல்லி
Centipede	puuraan	பூரான்
Snake	paampu	பாம்பு

Say in Tamil the English sentences given in the first column below:

English sentence	Tamil Equivalent using English script
We have a tortoise in our garden	naankall enkalludaiya thohddaththil oru aamai vaiththirukkirohm
There are spider webs all over	ellaa idamum silanthi valaihall irukkinrana

There is a snail on the wall	suvaril oru naththai irukkirathu
There are leeches in the forest	kaaddukkul̲ addaihal̲l̲ irukkinrana
There are many frogs near that pond	antha kullaththadiyil pala thavakkaihal̲l̲ irukkinrana
Here lizards are found everywhere	inkeh ellaa idamum pal-lihal̲l̲ kaanappadukinrana
Centipedes can be seen in Sri Lanka	ilankaiyil puuraankal̲l̲ai kaanalaam
This jungle is full of snakes	intha k-kaaddil nirraiya paampuhal̲l̲

EXERCISE 40

1. Write the Tamil words for the following and read them aloud.

    (i) garden   (ii) webs   (iii) wall
    (iv) pond   (v) everywhere   (vi) jungle

2. Read aloud the following:

இந்தியாவின் சுப்ரமணிய
பாரதியார் ஒரு மகா கவிஞர், எழுத்தாளர்,
இதழாளர், சமூகச் சீர்திருத்தச் சிந்தனையாளர்,
விடுதலைப் போராட்ட வீரர் எனப் பன்முக
ஆற்றல் கொண்டவர் ஆவார்.

LESSON 41

Crockery

Cup, Glass, Tumbler, Bottle, Plate, Spoon, Knife, Fork

English word	Tamil word written using English script	Tamil word written using Tamil script
Cup	kohppai	கோப்பை
Glass	kannaadi-p-paaththiram	கண்ணாடிப்பாத்திரம்
Tumbler	kudikkum kuva<u>ll</u>ai	குடிக்கும் குவளை
Bottle	pohththal	போத்தல்
Plate	thaddu	தட்டு
Spoon	karandi	கரண்டி
Knife	kaththi	கத்தி
Fork	mullukkarandi	முள்ளுக்கரண்டி

Say in Tamil the English sentences given in the first column below:

English sentence	Tamil Equivalent using English script
Please get me a cup of coffee	thayavuseithu enakku oru (kohppai) kohppi thaarunka<u>ll</u>
Keep the cup on the saucer	kohppaiyai peerisil vaiyunka<u>ll</u>

105

I need a bottle of water	enakku oru pohththal thanhnheer vehnum
Give me a glass of milk	enakku oru 'glass' paal thaarunka<u>ll</u>
Don't you have a metal tumbler?	unka<u>ll</u>idam oru 'metal' kudikkum kuva<u>ll</u>ai i<u>ll</u>aiyaa?
Bring the food in a plate	saappaaddai thaddil konduvaarunka<u>ll</u>
I will eat with a fork and a knife	naan kaththiyaalaiyum mullukkarandiyalaiyum saapiduvehn
Please give me a spoon	thayavu seythu enakku oru karandi thaarunka<u>ll</u>

> **EXERCISE 41**
>
> 1. Write the Tamil words for the following and read them aloud.
>
>   (i) get-me (ii) keep (iii) give-me
>   (iv) food (v) will-eat
>
> 2. Search 'YouTube' and listen to the Bharathi song:
>
>   ஓடி விளையாடு பாப்பா - நீ ஓய்ந்திருக்க லாகாது பாப்பா, கூடி விளையாடு பாப்பா, - ஒரு குழந்தையை வையாதே பாப்பா.
>
>   சின்னஞ் சிறுகுருவி போலே - நீ திரிந்து பறந்துவா பாப்பா, வண்ணப் பறவைகளைக் கண்டு - நீ மனதில் மகிழ்ச்சி கொள்ளு பாப்பா.
>
>   கொத்தித் திரியுமந்தக் கோழி - அதைக் கூட்டி விளையாடு பாப்பா, எத்தித் திருடுமந்தக் காக்காய் - அதற்கு இரக்கப் படவேணும் பாப்பா.

LESSON 42

Vegetables

Onion, Chilli, Tomato, Potato, Cabbage, Egg-plant, Okra, Beans, Radish, Cucumber, Drumstick

English word	Tamil word written using English script	Tamil word written using Tamil script
Onion	venkaayam	வெங்காயம்
Chilli	millakaayi	மிளகாய்
Tomato	thakkaalli	தக்காளி
Potato	urullaikkizhanku	உருளைக்கிழங்கு
Cabbage	kohvaa	கோவா
Egg-plant	kaththarikkaai	கத்தரிக்காய்
Okra	vendikkaai	வெண்டிக்காய்
Bean	pohnchi	போஞ்சி
Radish	mull llanki	முள்ளங்கி
Cucumber	vell llarikkaayi	வெள்ளரிக்காய்
Drumstick	murunkaikkaayi	முருங்கைக்காய்

Say in Tamil the English sentences given in the first column below:

English sentence	Tamil Equivalent using English script
How much is a kilo of onions?	Oru kilo venkaayam enna vilai?
Green chillies add taste to the cabbage curry	Pachchai milakaayi kova karikku urusai kodukkirathu

Okra and drumstick are my favourite vegetables	Vedikkaayum murunkaikkaayum ennudaiya virupamaana kaaikarika<u>ll</u>
Tomatoes are good for the heart	Thakkaazhi iruthayathukku nal-lathu
Today mum is cooking bean curry	Inraikku ammah pohnchikkaayi samaikra
We need some cucumber for the salad	'salad' ikkup pohda enkalukku koncham ve<u>ll</u>-<u>ll</u>arikkaayi thehvai
Radish is readily available here	mu<u>ll</u> <u>ll</u>anki inkeh ilahuvaakak kidaikkum

EXERCISE 42

1. Write the Tamil words for the following and read them aloud.

   (i) taste   (ii) favourite   (iii) vegetables
   (iv) heart   (v) cooking   (vi) need

2. Search 'YouTube' and listen to the nursery rhyme:

"நான் சின்னப்பெண்ணான போதிலே…."

LESSON 43

Fruits

Orange, Grape, Apple, Banana, Mango, Coconut, Jack fruit

English word	Tamil word written using English script	Tamil word written using Tamil script
Orange	thohdampazham	தோடம்பழம்
Grape	munthirihaippazham	முந்திரிகைப்பழம்
Apple	aappillpazham	ஆப்பிள்பழம்
Banana	vaazhaippazham	வாழைப்பழம்
Mango	maampazham	மாம்பழம்
Coconut	thehnkaayi	தேங்காய்
Jack fruit	palaa-p-pazham	பலாப்பழம்

Say in Tamil the English sentences given in the first column below:

English sentence	Tamil Equivalent using English script
I must buy some oranges today	naan inraikku koncha thohdampazham vaanka vehnum
Grapes are very expensive	munthirihaippazham athiha vilai
Apples are good for health	'apples' aarohkkiaththukku nal-lathu
Banana is my favourite fruit	vaazhaippazham enakku viruppamaana pazham
This is not the mango season	ithu maampazha-k-kaalamal-la
Coconut milk adds taste to any curry	thehnkaayi paal entha-k-karikkum urusai tharum
Jack fruit is very tasty	palaa-p-pazham nal-la urusai

EXERCISE 43

1. Write the Tamil words for the following and read them aloud.

   (i) buy   (ii) expensive   (iii) health   (iv) fruit
   (v) season   (vi) milk

2. Write each sentence in the table above in Tamil script and read it aloud.

LESSON 44

Seafood

Fish, Dried fish, Prawn, Crab, Squid, Cuttlefish

English word	Tamil word written using English script	Tamil word written using Tamil script
Fish	meen	மீன்
Dried fish	karuvaadu	கருவாடு
Prawn	iraal	இறால்
Crab	nanhdu	நண்டு
Squid	uusi kanhavaai	ஊசி கணவாய்
Cuttlefish	kanhavaai	கணவாய்

Say in Tamil the English sentences given in the first column below:

English sentence	Tamil equivalent using English script
Fish is generally good for health	meen pothuvaaha aarohkkiaththukku nal-lathu
I love prawn curry	enakku iraal karri nal-la viruppam
Most people like both prawn and crab curries	athihappehr iraal, nandhu karri irandaiyum virumpuhiraarha_ll_.

Dried fish is exported by Sri Lanka	ilankaiyil irunthu karuvaadu ehttrumathi seyyappadukirathu
Cuttlefish is much tastier than squid	kanavaai uusi kanhavaayilum paarkka mihavum urusaiyaanathu

EXERCISE 44

1. What are the Tamil words for the following?

   (i) generally (ii) most-people (iii) both
   (iv) exports (v) tastier

2. Read the following aloud.

   ஒளவையார் (Avvaiyaar) நன்கு அறிமுகமான ஒரு பெண் புலவர்.
   ஒளவை என்பது மூதாட்டி அல்லது தவப்பெண் என்ற கருத்தை உடையது. ஒளவையின் கவிதைகளில் ஒன்று கீழே தரப்பட்டுள்ளது:

   "நெல்லுக்கிறைத்த நீர்வாய்க்கால் வழியோடி
   புல்லுக்கும் ஆங்கே பொசியுமாம்.
   தொல்லுலகில் நல்லார் ஒருவர் உளரேல்
   அவர்பொருட்டு எல்லோர்க்கும் பெய்யும் மழை."

   Meaning in English:

   "In the paddy field the water routed to the paddy also goes to the grass that grows there.

   If there is one good person in the universe, it will rain for everyone because of them."

LESSON 45

Meats

Beef, Mutton, Lamb, Pork, Chicken

English word	Tamil word written using English script	Tamil word written using Tamil script
Beef	maaddiraichchi	மாட்டிறைச்சி
Mutton / Goat meat	aaddiraichchi	ஆட்டிறைச்சி
Lamb	kuddiaaddu iraichchi	குட்டிஆட்டு இறைச்சி
Pork	panri iraichchi	பன்றி இறைச்சி
Chicken meat	kohli iraichchi	கோழி இறைச்சி

Say in Tamil the English sentences given in the first column below:

English sentence	Tamil Equivalent using English script
This beef preparation is delicious	intha maaddiraichchi thayaarippu nal-la urusi
I prefer goat curry to lamb	naan kuddi aaddu iraichchiyai vida aaddiraichchiyai kuuda virumpukirehn
My friend won't eat beef	ennudaiya nanhpan maaddiraichchi saappidamaaddaar

Pork is not eaten by many people	panri iraichchiyai palapehr saappiduvathil-lai
My mother cooks very tasty chicken curry	ennudaiya ammah nalla urusaiyaana kohli iraichchi 'curry' samaippaa
We shall buy some chicken nuggets today	inru naanka<u>ll</u> koncha 'chicken nuggets' vaankuvohm

EXERCISE 45

1. Write the Tamil words for the following and read them aloud.

    (i) preparation   (ii) delicious   (iii) prefer
    (iv) friend   (v) eat   (vi) cooks

2. Write in Tamil, a sentence involving each of the words above.
  (You may use the appropriate sentence as seen in the table above).

LESSON 46

Stationery

Pen, Pencil, Eraser, Ruler, Sharpener, Clip, Stapler

English word	Tamil word written using English script	Tamil word written using Tamil script
Pen	pehnai	பேனை
Pencil	pensil	பென்சில்*
Eraser (Rubber)	irappar	இறப்பர்
Ruler	adimaddam	அடிமட்டம்
Sharpener	saappinhar	'சாப்பிணர்' *
Clip	clip	கிளிப் *
Stapler	stapler	ஸ்ரேப்லர் *

* No commonly used Tamil words for these

No matter how hard you push the pencil it's still stationery!

எழுதக் கிற, வெட்ட அழிக்க உதவும் பொருள்கள்

Say in Tamil the English sentences given in the first column below:

English sentence	Tamil Equivalent using English script
Can I borrow your pen for some time?	naan unkalludaiya pehnaiyai koncha nehram kadan vaankalaamaa?
Have you got a pencil?	unkallidam oru pencil irukkuthaa?
Give me an eraser	enakku oru irappar thaarum
You will need a ruler	unkallukku oru adimaddam thehvaippadum
Can you sharpen that pencil?	antha pensilai kuurmaiaakkuveeraa?
You must get yourself a pencil sharpener.	neenkall oru 'pencil sharpener' ai-p pettukkollavehnum
We need a stapler or a paper clip.	enkalukku oru 'stapler' allathu oru kadathaasi 'clip' thehvai

---

EXERCISE 46

1. What are the Tamil words for the following?

   (i) borrow (ii) give me (iii) need
   (iv) ruler (v) get-yourself

2. Write in Tamil, a sentence involving each of the words above.
   (You may use the appropriate sentence as seen in the table above).

LESSON 47

Money Dealings

Cheap, Dear, Discount, Commission, Brokerage, Donation

English	Tamil word written using English script	Tamil word written using Tamil script
Cheap	malivu	மலிவு
Dear	athiha vilai	அதிக விலை
Discount	vilai tha<u>ll</u> <u>l</u>upadi	விலை தள்ளுபடி
Commission	komisan	கொமிசன் *
Brokerage	'broker' komisan	புரோக்கர் கொமிசன்*
Donation	nan kodai	நன் கொடை

*No spoken Tamil words for these

Say in Tamil the English sentences given in the first column below:

English sentence	Tamil Equivalent using English script
I bought this very cheap	naan ithai nal-la malivaaha vaankinehn
Motor cars are not very dear	mohttaar vaahanankal<u>l</u> athika vilai al-la
I received a very good discount	enakku nal-la vilai tha<u>ll</u> <u>l</u>upadi kidaiththathu

117

I had to pay a commission for that transaction	naan antha kodukkal vaankalukku komisan kodukka vehndi irunthathu
The brokerage fee for this transaction is very high	intha kodukkal vaankalukku 'broker' komisan mikka athiham
I made a big donation for that charity	naan antha tharmaththukku periya nan-kodai seythehn

EXERCISE 47

1. What are the Tamil words for the following?

    (i) bought   (ii) received   (iii) transaction
    (iv) big

2. Write in Tamil, a sentence involving each of the words above.

    (You may use an appropriate sentence as seen in the table above).

LESSON 48

Institutions

School, College, Hospital, Church, Temple, Police Station, University, Airport

English word	Tamil word written using English script	Tamil word written using Tamil script
School	pa<u>ll</u> <u>ll</u>ikuudam	பள்ளிக்கூடம்
College	kal-luuri	கல்லூரி
Hospital	aaspaththiri	ஆஸ்பத்திரி
Church	thehvaalayam	தேவாலயம்
Temple	kohvil	கோவில்
Police Station	polis nilaiyam	பொலிஸ் நிலையம்
University	palkalaikkazhaham	பல்கலைக்கழகம்
Airport	vimaana nilaiyam	விமான நிலையம்

Say in Tamil the English sentences given in the first column below:

English sentence	Tamil Equivalent using English script
Which school does your son go to?	ummudaiya pi<u>ll</u> <u>ll</u>ai entha pa<u>ll</u> <u>ll</u>ikkuudaththukku pohkiraar?
I studied in two colleges	naan irandu kal-luuriha<u>ll</u>il padiththehn

How far is the nearest hospital from your home?	ummudaiya veeddukkukkidda ulla aaspaththiri evvalavu thuuram?
Is there a catholic church around here?	ivvidaththil kaththohlikka thehvaalayam onru irukkirathaa?
I see many protestant churches here.	naan inku pala 'protestant' thehvaalayankallai paarkirehn
There is a Buddhist temple at the end of this road	inthath-theruvin kadaisiyil oru puththa kohvil irukkirathu
The police station is quite far from here	Polis nilaiyam inkirunthu konchath-thuuram
Gowri is a lecturer at the Colombo University	'Gowri' kolumpu palkalaikkazhahaththil oru virivuraiaalar
We have a very big airport.	enkallidam oru mihapperiya vimaana nilaiyam irukkirathu

EXERCISE 48

1. What are the Tamil words for the following?

    (i) studied   (ii) many   (iii) far
    (iv) churches (v) lecturer (vi) very big

2. Write in Tamil, a sentence involving each of the words above.

    (You may use an appropriate sentence as seen in the table above).

LESSON 49

Modes of Transport

Car, Train, Bus, Coach, Plane, Helicopter

English word	Tamil word written using English script	Tamil word written using Tamil script
Car	kaar (mohttaar vanhdi)	கார் (மோட்டார் வண்டி)
Train	puhai-iratham (puhai vanhdi)	புகையிரதம் (புகை வண்டி)
Bus (Coach)	pas vanhdi	பஸ் வண்டி
Plane	aakaaya vimaanam	ஆகாய விமானம்
Helicopter	'helicopter'	கெலிக்கொப்ரர் / உலங்கு வானூர்தி

Say in Tamil the English sentences given in the first column below:

English sentence	Tamil Equivalent using English script
I bought a new car last week	naan pohna kizhamai oru puthu 'car' vaankinehn
I go by the 7.30 AM train to work	naan vehlaikku kaalai 7.30 mani puhai iratha vanhdiyaal pohvehn

Is there a bus to Colombo from here?	inkirunthu kozhumpukku oru 'bus' irukkuthaa?
My brother is arriving today by plane	ennudaiya sahohtharar inru vimaanaththaal varukiraar
I enjoyed the helicopter ride yesterday	nehtru naan 'helicopter' savaariyai anupaviththehn

EXERCISE 49

1. What are the Tamil words for the following?

    (i) last week   (ii) from here   (iii) arriving   (iv) enjoyed

2. Write in Tamil, a sentence involving each of the words above.
    (you may use an appropriate sentence as seen in the table above).

பஸ் வண்டி

LESSON 50

Locations

Town, Village, City, Country, Rural, Urban

English word	Tamil word written using English script	Tamil word written using Tamil script
Town	nakaram	நகரம்
Village	kiraamam	கிராமம்
City	maanakaram	மாநகரம்
Country	naadu	நாடு
Rural	kiraamiya	கிராமிய
Urban	nakaram chaarntha	நகரம் சார்ந்த

Say in Tamil the English sentences given in the first column below:

English sentence	Tamil Equivalent using English script
I grew up in a small town	naan oru siru nakaraththil vallarnthehn
Rajah is from a small village near Kandy	"Rajah" kandikku kidda ull lla kiraamaththavar
There is a lot of fun activity in the city at nights	maa-nakaraththil iravuhalil pala kehlikkai sampavankall irukkinrana

123

Our country is quite peaceful	enka<u>ll</u>udaiya naadu ohralavu samaathaanamaanathu
The people in the rural areas have a distinct culture	kiraamiya makka<u>ll</u>ukku oru thani kalaachaaram irukkirathu
Most people like to work in the urban areas.	athihamaana aadka<u>ll</u> naharam chaarntha idankalil vehlai seyya virumpuvar

EXERCISE 50

1. What are the Tamil words for the following?

    (i) small (ii) activity (iii) peaceful
    (iv) culture (v) work

2. Write in Tamil, a sentence involving each of the words.
   (You may use an appropriate sentence as seen in the table above).

3. Two epic poems of ancient India are Mahaabharata and Raamaayana. Read aloud the following regarding Mahaabharata.

   மகாபாரதம் என்பது அனைத்து காலத்து மக்களையும் அறிவூட்டும் வகையில் அமைந்த சிறந்த மதிப்புமிக்க படைப்புகளில் ஒன்றாகும். இது பல குறிப்பிடத்தக்க உண்மைகளுடன் அமைந்துள்ளது. ஒரு மனிதனின் வாழ்க்கைக்கு தேவையான மனித நேயம் மற்றும் நெறிமுறைகளைக் கற்றுக் கொள்ள மகாபாரதம் மிகவும் உதவுகிறது. மனிதர்கள் என்பவர்கள் ஒரு சமூக விலங்குகள் போன்றவர்கள் அவர்கள் சமூகத்தின் விதிகளுக்கு கட்டுப்பட வேண்டும். இந்த உண்மை மகாபாரதத்தின் சிறுகதைகளில் தெளிவாக நிறுவப்பட்டுள்ளது.

LESSON 51

Gardens

Garden, Park, Grass, Plant, Weed, Flower

English word	Tamil word written using English script	Tamil word written using Tamil script
Garden	thohddam	தோட்டம்
Park	puunkaavanam	பூங்காவனம்
Grass	pul	புல்
Plant	chedi	செடி
Weed	kallai	களை
Flower	malar/puu	மலர் / பூ

Say in Tamil the English sentences given in the first column below:

English sentence	Tamil Pronunciation using English script
You have a beautiful front garden	unkallidam munnukku azhahaana thohddam irukirathu
There is a public park near our house	pothup puunkaavanam onru enkall veeddukku aruhhil ull llathu
That grass looks very nice	antha pul paarvaikku arumaiyaaka irukkirathu

There are many plants in your garden	unka<u>ll</u>udaiya thohddaththil pala sediha<u>ll</u> irukkinrana
I need to spray my plants with weed killer	naan ennudaiya sedihalukku ka<u>ll</u>ai naasini the<u>ll</u>ikka vehnum
I must buy some flowers for my wife	naan eennudaiya manaivikku koncha puu vaanka vehnum

EXERCISE 51

1. What are the Tamil words for the following?

   (i) front (ii) near (iii) very nice (iv) garden (v) weed-killer (vi) wife

2. Write in Tamil, a sentence involving each of the words above.
   (You may use an appropriate sentence as seen in the table above).

3. Read aloud the following regarding Ramayana.

   ராமாயணம் என்பது ஒரு பழங்கால சமஸ்கிருத காவியமாகும். இளவரசர் ராமர் தனது மனைவி சீதையை இராவணனின் பிடியிலிருந்து மீட்பதற்கு அனுமன் படையின் உதவியுடன் தன் தேடலைத் தொடங்கினார். இந்த காவியத்தின் கதை கிமு 500 முதல் கிமு 100 வரை நடைபெற்றது. இதனை பாரம்பரியமான முறையில் வால்மீகி முனிவர் இயற்றியுள்ளார்.

LESSON 52

Spices

Mustard, Turmeric, Garlic, Ginger, Chilli powder, Curry Powder, Cinnamon

English word	Tamil word written using English script	Tamil word written using Tamil script
Mustard	kaduhu	கடுகு
Turmeric	manchall	மஞ்சள்
Garlic	ulli / vellai puundu	உள்ளி / வெள்ளை ப்பூண்டு
Ginger	inchi	இஞ்சி
Chilli powder	millakaayi-th-thool	மிளகாய்த்தூள்
Curry powder	karri-th- thool	கறித்தூள்
Cinnamon	karruvaa	கறுவா

Say in Tamil the English sentences given in the first column below:

English sentence	Tamil Equivalent using English script
I use mustard for my curries	naan enathu karihallukku kaduhu paavippehn
Too much of tumeric is not good for health	athika manchall, udal nalaththukku nal-lathal-la
Garlic is available in the form of paste	ull lli, pasai ruupaththil kidaikkakuudiyathaha ull llathu

Ginger is an essential ingredient for Asian cooking	inchi aasia samaiyalukku aththiyaavasiyamaana sey poru<u>ll</u>.
Chilli powder is used for most Indian curries	anehkamaana inthian karriha<u>ll</u>ukku mi<u>ll</u>akaayi-th-thoo<u>ll</u> paavikkappadukirathu
Curry powder can be used with chilli powder	karri-th- thoo<u>ll</u>ai mi<u>ll</u>akaayi-th-thoo<u>ll</u>udan kalanthu paavikkalaam
Cinnamon is used to give flavour to curries.	karriha<u>ll</u>ukku vaasanai thara karruvaa paavikkappaduhirathu

EXERCISE 52

1. What are the Tamil words for the following?

   (i) health   (ii) essential   (iii) most
   (iv) used   (v) flavour

2. Write in Tamil, a sentence involving each of the words above.

(You may use an appropriate sentence as seen in the table above).

மிளகும் உப்பும்

LESSON 53

Persons

People, Man, Woman, Children, Pupil, Student

English word	Tamil word written using English script	Tamil word written using Tamil script
People	maka<u>ll</u>	மக்கள்
Man	manithan	மனிதன்
Woman	manusi	மனுசி
Children	pi<u>ll</u> <u>ll</u>aiha<u>ll</u>	பிள்ளைகள்
Pupil / Student	pa<u>ll</u> <u>ll</u>i maanhavar / maanhavar	பள்ளி மாணவர் / மாணவர்

Say in Tamil the English sentences given in the first column below:

English sentence	Tamil Pronunciation using English script
People are happy with the present government	maka<u>ll</u> thattkaala arasaankkaththudan mahizhchiyaaha irukkiraarha<u>ll</u>
Man is the head of a family	manithan oru kudumpaththin thalaivan
Some women occupy very high positions in workplaces	sila penhha<u>ll</u> uththiyohka idanka<u>ll</u>il mihapperiya pathaviha<u>ll</u>il irukkiraarha<u>ll</u>
Children have too much freedom these days	intha naadka<u>ll</u>il pi<u>ll</u> <u>ll</u>aika<u>ll</u>ukku athihamaana sutha<u>n</u>thiram irukirathu

There are more than a thousand pupils in this school	intha pa<u>ll</u>ikkuudaththil aayiraththukku mehlaana pa<u>ll</u> lli maanhavarha<u>ll</u> irukkiraarha<u>ll</u>
University students are under a lot of stress	palkalaikkazhaha maanhavarha<u>ll</u>ukku niraiya manavulaichchal

EXERCISE 53

1. What are the Tamil words for the following?

    (i) government   (ii) family   (iii) freedom   (iv) stress

2. Write in Tamil, a sentence involving each of the words above.
   (You may use an appropriate sentence as seen in the table above).

3. Read aloud the Na<u>ll</u>an- Damayanthi story below.

   நளன் நிடத நாட்டை ஆண்டு வந்தான். இவனுடைய மனைவி தமயந்தி. மகிழ்ச்சியுடன் குறைவற்ற வாழ்வு வாழ்ந்துவந்தான். அயல் நாட்டு அரசனுடன் சூது விளையாட்டில் ஈடுபட்டுத் தனது நாட்டை இழந்தான். நாட்டை விட்டு வெளியேறிய அவனுடன் தானும் வருவேன் எனத் தமயந்தி பிடிவாதமாகச் சென்றாள். தனது மனைவி கல்லிலும் முள்ளிலும் நடந்து துன்பப் படுவது கண்டு பொறாத நளன், வழியிலேயே அவளைக் கைவிட்டுச் சென்று விடுகிறான். அதன் பின்னர் பல ஆண்டுகள் அவனுக்கு துன்பங்கள் ஏற்பட்டு, இறுதியில் மீண்டும் அவன் இழந்த அரசைப்பெற்று மனைவியுடன் மகிழ்ச்சியாய் வாழ்ந்தான்.

LESSON 54

Office Accessories

Books, Basket, Tray, Bookshelf, Cabinet, Files, Folders

English word	Tamil word written using English script	Tamil word written using Tamil script
Book	puththakam	புத்தகம்
Basket	kuudai	கூடை
Tray	thaampaallam/ thaddu	தாம்பாளம் / தட்டு
Bookshelf	puththaha thaddu	புத்தக த்தட்டு
Cabinet	nilai-p-peddi / alumaari	நிலைப்பெட்டி / அலுமாரி
Files/folders	kohppuhal	கோப்புகள்

Say in Tamil the English sentences given in the first column below:

English sentence	Tamil Equivalent using English script
I borrowed that book from the library	naan antha puththakaththai noolahaththil iraval vaankinehn
Put those documents in the basket	antha aavanhangkalai kuudaiyil pohdavum
There are a lot of unattended letters in that tray	anthaththaddil oru thohai kavanikkappadaatha kadithankal̲l̲ irukkinrana

131

My bookshelf needs to be arranged properly	ennudaiya puththaha nilai-p-peddiyai sariyaana muraiyil ozhunkupaduththa vehnum
We shall move the filing cabinet to the other corner.	naanka<u>ll</u> nilai-p-peddiyai matra muulaikku naharththuvohm
Please open the relevant files	thayavu seythu sampanthappadda kohppuhalai thirakkavum
Keep all the new documents in this folder	puthiya aavanhangka<u>ll</u>ai intha kohppil vaikkavum

EXERCISE 54

1. What are the Tamil words for the following?

   (i) library (ii) documents (iii) unattended
   (iv) arranged (v) move (vi) files

2. Write in Tamil, a sentence involving each of the words.
   (You may use an appropriate sentence as seen in the table above).

3. Read aloud the following Passage:

   தீபாவளி (Deepavali, Diwali) அல்லது தீப ஒளித்திருநாள் என்பது ஐந்து நாட்கள் ஐப்பசி / கார்த்திகை மாதங்களில் கொண்டாடப்படுகின்ற பண்டிகையாகும்.
   இப்பண்டிகை இந்தியா இலங்கை சிங்கப்பூர் உட்பட பல நாடுகளில் கொண்டாடப்படுகிறது. வாழ்க்கையின் இருளை நீக்கி, ஒளியைக் கொடுக்கும் பண்டிகையாக தீபாவளிப் பண்டிகை கொண்டாடப்படுகிறது.

LESSON 55

Rates Of Motion

Slow, Fast, Slowly, Faster, Speed, Accelerate

English word	Tamil word written using English script	Tamil word written using Tamil script
Slow	mel-lamaaha / methuvaaha	மெல்லமாக / மெதுவாக
Fast	viraivaaha / thurithamaaha	விரைவாக / துரிதமாக
Slowly	Innum mel-lamaaha / innum methuvaaha	இன்னும் மெல்லமாக / இன்னும் மெதுவாக
Faster	innum viraivaaha / innum thurithamaaha	இன்னும் விரைவாக / இன்னும் துரிதமாக
Speed	vehkam	வேகம்
Accelerate	vehkamuuddu	வேகமூட்டு

Say in Tamil the English sentences given in the first column below:

English sentence	Tamil Equivalent using English script
Please go slow	thayavuseythu mellamaaha pohkavum

You speak so fast	neenka_ll_ sariyaana thurithamaaha katha ikireerka_ll_
They are slowly catching up with us	avarha_ll_ methuvaaha enka_ll_ai pidikkiraarha_ll_
Drive a little faster	innum koncham viraivaaha ohddum
Speed kills	vehkam kol-lum
There is no way we can accelerate on this road	inthath-theruvil vehkamuudduthal iyalaathu

EXERCISE 55

1. What are the Tamil words for the following?

    (i) speak   (ii) catching   (iii) little   (iv) road

2. Write in Tamil, a sentence involving each of the words above.
(You may use an appropriate sentence as seen in the table above).

LESSON 56

Conversation (1) – Going Shopping

Friend: **Are you going shopping today?**
neenka__ll__ indaikku kadaikkup pohhireerha__ll__aa?

Me: **Yes.**
ohm.

Friend: **What time are you planning to go?**
eththanai manikku neenka__ll__ pohha yohsikkireerha__ll__?

Me: **Say, around 10 AM.**
kaalamai paththu manhi pohla.

Friend: **Would you be able to take me?**
ennai kuuddikondu poha mudiyumaa?

Me: **Yes, sure. I will come at ten.**
ohm athukkenna. naan paththu manikku varuvehn.

Friend: **That will be good. I will be ready at ten. See you later.**
athu nallathu. naan paththukku aayaththamaayi iruppehn. pirahu kaanuvohm.

LESSON 57

Conversation (2) – Getting A Taxi

Passenger: **How much is the fare to go to the airport?**
vimaana nilaiyaththukkup pohka evvalavu kaasu?

Driver: **It is about Rs14,000.**
kiddaththadda pathinaalaayiram ruupaa.

Passenger: **How long would it take to get there?**
anku pohka evvalavu nehram edukkum?

Driver: **It would take approximately one hour and 45 minutes along Colombo Road.**
Kolumpu rohddaalai pohnaal kiddaththadda oru manhiththiyaalam naatpathayinthu nimidankall edukkum.

Passenger: **Is there any faster route to get there?**
anku pohvathatrku vehru viraivaana paathai itukkirathaa?

Driver: **No, this is the quickest.**
Il-lai. ithuthaan kethiyaanathu.

Passenger: **Okay, let's go.**
sari, pohvam.

Passenger: **Could you please turn to the right here and then to the left and stop at the entrance?**
thayavuseythu ingeh valathu pakkam thirumpi, pirahu idathu pakkam thirumpi, vaasalil nitrpaaddunka<u>ll</u>?

Driver: **Okay.**
sari.

Passenger: **Thank you, stay safe.**
upahaaram. Paathuhaappaaha irunka<u>ll</u>

Driver: **Thank you and wish you a safe journey.**
upahaaram. suhap-payanhathukku vaazhththukkall.

LESSON 58

Conversation (3) – Checking in at the Airport

Airline staff: **Good morning, Can I have your ticket, please?**
kaalai vanhakkam. thayavu seythu unka<u>ll</u> pirayaana cheeddaith thara mudiyumaa?

Passenger: **Please give me a window seat.**
ohm, thayavu seythu jannal pakkamaaha 'seat' tharuveerha<u>ll</u>a?

Airline staff: **Possible.**
tharalaam.

Airline staff: **Is there any baggage?**
'baggage" ehthaavathu irukkirathaa?

Passenger: **Yes, a suitcase and a hand bag.**
ohm. otu 'suitcase' um, otu 'handbag' um.

Airline staff: **Did you pack your bag yourself?**
unka<u>ll</u>udaiya 'bag'ai neenka<u>ll</u> than adukkineerha<u>ll</u>a?

Passenger: **Yes.**
ohm.

Airline staff: **Is there any dangerous chemicals in the bag?**
'bag' ikku<u>ll</u> ehthaavathu aapaththaana irasaayana porudka<u>ll</u> irukkirathaa?

Passenger: **No.**
Il-lai.

Airline staff: **Here's your boarding pass, enjoy your flight.**
intharunka<u>ll</u>
unka<u>ll</u>'boarding pass'.
'flight' ai anupaviyunka<u>ll</u>.

Passenger: **Thank you.**
Nanri.

LESSON 59

Conversation (4) – Getting a Room in a Hotel

Hotel staff:	**Good evening, Can I help you?** maalai vanakkam. naan (umakku) uthava mudiyumaa?
Guest:	**Yes please. I would like a room for the night.** ohm. enakku iravukku oru arai vehnum.
Hotel staff:	**Would you like a single room, or a double room?** unkallukku thani arraiyaa al-lathu iraddai araiyaa vehnum?
Guest:	**A single room. How much is the room?** 'thani arrai'. arraikku evvalavu kaasu?
Hotel staff:	**It's Rs. 14, 900 per night.** oru iravukku pathinaalaayiraththi thozhaayiram ruupaa.
Guest:	**Can I pay by credit card?** naan 'credit card' aal 'pay' panna mudiyumaa?
Hotel staff:	**Certainly. We take Visa, Master Card and American Express. Could you fill in this form, please?** ohm. naankall 'Visa', 'Master card' al-lathu 'American Express card.'eduppohm. thayavu seythu intha paththiraththai nirappireerhalaa?
Guest:	**Do you need my passport ?** unkallukku ennudaiya 'passport' thehvaiyaa?
Hotel staff:	**No, just the name, address, and your signature.** Il-lai, peyarum, vilaasamum, unkalludaiya kai ezhluththum maaththiramthaan.
Guest:	(fills out the form) **Here you are, the filled form.** inthaarunkall nirappiya paththiram.

Hotel staff:	**Here's the room key. Room number is 22. You can see the beech from your room.** inthaarunka<u>ll</u> arai-ch-chaavi. arai ilakkam irupaththi irandu. araiyilirunthu paarka 'beach' theriyum.
Guest:	**Thank you very much.** mikka nanri.
Hotel staff:	**If you need anything, dial 0 on the telephone.** ehthaavathu thehvai enraal, tholai pehsiyil 'zero' vai azhaiyunka<u>ll</u>.
Guest:	(calls room service) **I am calling from room 22. Could I please have a bottle of Port wine.** naan irupaththi irandaam ilakka araiyilirunthu kooppiduhirehn. enakku oru pohththal 'Port wine' thara mudiyumaa?
Hotel staff:	**Yes madam, your order will be there in 10 minutes.** ohm ammah, unkall 'order' paththu nimidaththil varum.
Guest:	**Thank you very much.** mikka nanri.

LESSON 60

Conversation (5) – Having a Meal in a Restaurant

Waitress: **Good afternoon, here is the menu for today, sir.**
mathiya vanakkam, aiyaa ithu inraya 'menu'.

Customer: **Thank you. What's today's special?**
nanri. inraikku enna 'special'?

Waitress: **Mutton Buriyani and Vattalappam.**
aaddu buriyaanium vattalappamum.

Customer: **That sounds good. I'll have that.**
athu nallathu. naan athai edukkirehn.

Waitress: **Would you like something to drink?**
unkalukkuk kudikka ehthaavathu vehnumaa?

Customer: **Yes, give me a beer.**
ohm. enakku oru 'beer' thaarunkall.

Waitress: (hands over the beer) **Let me know when you are ready to have the meal.**
saappida 'ready' enraal enakku sol-lunkall.

Customer: **Shall do. Thank you.**
solluhirehn, nanri.

Waitress: **Here is your meal sir. Enjoy.**
inthaarunkall unkall saappaadu. rasiyunkall.

Customer: **May I have the bill, please?**
thayavuseythu 'bill' ai thaarreerakallaa?

Waitress: **Here is the bill, sir.**
Inthaanrunkall aiyaa 'bill'.

Customer:	**Here is the money. Keep the change!** inthaarunka<u>ll</u> kaasu. michchaththai vaithirunka<u>ll</u>!
Waitress:	**Thank you. See you again.** nanri, aduththamurai kaanhuvohm.

LESSON 61

Conversation (6) - Getting Traveller's Cheques

Forex Teller: **Good Morning, how may I help you?**
kaalai vanakkam. naan unka*ll*ukku eppadi uthavalaam?

Customer: **I would like to cash some travellers' cheques.**
naan koncha 'travellers' cheques' maatra virumpuhirehn.

Forex Teller: **In what currency have you got them? Can I have the cheques and your passport please?**
enna kaasu vaichchirukkirreerka*ll*? thayavuseythu 'cheques' aiyum unkalludaiya 'passport' aiyum thara mudiyumaa?

Customer: **Here you are, the travellers' cheques are in American dollars.**
inthaarunka*ll*, 'travellers' cheques' American dollaril itukkirathu.

Forex Teller: **How much are you cashing?**
evvalavai neenkall maathirreerkall?

Customer: **I would like to cash 300 American dollars.**
naan mun-nuuru 'American dollars' maaththa virumpukirehn.

Forex Teller: **In what denominations would you like to have the cash?**
kaasai unka*ll*ukku enna nohddukalil vehnum?

Customer: **Give me half in 5-thousand-rupee notes, some thousand-rupee notes and the rest in 100's.**
araivaasiyai aiyaayirm ruupaa nohddilum, konchaththai aayiram ruupaa nohddilum, mihuthiyai nuuru rupaavilum thaarunka*ll*.

Forex Teller:	**Could you please sign each cheque for me?** thayavuseythu ovvoru 'cheque' ilum kai ezhuththup-p- pohduhireerkalaa?
Customer:	**Okay.** Sari.
Forex Teller:	**Here is the money. Have a nice day.** inthaarunka<u>ll</u> unka<u>ll</u> kaasu. nal vaazhthukka<u>ll</u>.
Customer:	**Thank you very much.** mikka nanri.

LESSON 62

Conversation (7) – Asking Directions to Market

Tourist: Is there a supermarket around here?
ivvidaththil oru 'supermarket' irukkirathaa?

Native: Yes. There's one near here.
ohm. kiddadiyil ondu irukkirathu.

Tourist: How do I get there?
naan anku eppadi pohvathu?

Native: Proceed along this street. At the first traffic lights, take a left and go straight on. It's on the right.
intha-p-paathaiyil pohnka_ll_. muthalaavathu 'traffic light' il idappakkamaaha thirumpi, pinpu nehra pohnka_ll_. athu valappakkaththil irukkirathu.

Tourist: Is it far?
thuuramaa?

Native: Not really.
Avvalavu thuuramil-lai

Tourist: Thank you.
nanri.

LESSON 63

Conversation (8) – Shopping for a Shirt

Shopkeeper: **Can I help you?**
                        naan uthavi seyya muidiyumaa?

Customer: **Yes, I'm looking for a gent's cotton shirt.**
                        ohm. naan aanhkalukku oru 'cotton shirt' paarkkirehn.

Shopkeeper: **What size are you after?**
                        Unka<u>ll</u>ukku enna 'size'vehnum?

Customer: **I want an large size.**
                        enakku oru periya 'size' vehnum.

Shopkeeper: **How about this one?**
                        ithu eppadi?

Customer: **Yes, that's nice. Can I try it on?**
                        ohm. athu nal-lathu. naan pohddup paarkkalaamaa?

Shopkeeper: **Good, there's the changing room over there.**
                        nal-lathu. udai maatrum arrai anku irukkirathu.

Customer: **Thank you.**
                        Nanri.

Shopkeeper: **How does it fit?**
                        eppadi a<u>ll</u>avu?

Customer: **It's a bit large. Do you have a smaller size?**
                        ithu koncham perisu. unka<u>ll</u>idam siriya 'size' irukkirathaa?

Shopkeeper: **Yes, here you are.**
                        ohm, inthaarum.

Customer:	**Thank you. I'll have it, please.** nanri. thayavuseythu ithaith thaarum.
Shopkeeper:	**OK, how would you like to pay?** nal-lathu. eppadi 'pay' panna virumpuhireerka<u>ll</u>?
Customer:	**Do you take credit card?** neenka<u>ll</u> 'credit card' eduppeerkalaa?
Shopkeeper:	**Yes, we take Visa, Master Card and American Express.** ohm, naanka<u>ll</u> Visa, Master card matrum 'American Express' eduppohm.
Customer:	**OK, here's my Visa card.** sari, inthaarunka<u>ll</u> enathu 'Visa card'.
Shopkeeper:	**Thank you.** nanri.

LESSON 64

Conversation (9) – Shopping Vegetables & Fruits

Vendor: **What vegetables would you like?**
enna marakkarrikal̲ unkal̲lukku viruppam?

Customer: (points at one) **how much does this vegetable cost?**
intha marakkarri enna vilai?

Vendor: **It costs Rs. 200 per kilo.**
ithu kilo irunuuru ruupai.

Customer: **How much are the drumsticks?**
murunkaikaai enna vilai?

Vendor: **Rs.250 for half kilo.**
arai kilo irunuutri ayimpathu ruupaa.

Vendor: **Would you like egg plant and spinach? They are very fresh.**
unkal̲lukku kaththariyum keeraiyum vehnumaa? avai nal-la puthusu.

Customer: **No, I would like to get a kilo each of the beans, potatoes, and onions.**
il-lai. naan 'beans', kizhangu, venhkaayam ovvonrilum ovvoru kilo vaanka virumpuhirehn.

Vendor: **Will that be all?**
avvaluvum thaanaa?

Customer: **No, I would like some fruits as well.**
il-lai, naan koncha pazhankal̲lum (vaanka)virumpuhirehn.

Vendor: **There are ripe tasty mangoes, bananas, red apples, wood apple, pineapple, and green papaw, what would you like?**

nal-la pazhuththa urusiyaana maampazham, vaalaipazham, sivappu aaple, vizhaampalam, annaasi pachchai pappa aahiyavai irukkirathu. unkalluku ethu virupam?

Customer: **Please give me a kilo each of all the fruits except the papaw.**
thayavuseythu pappaavai thavira mattra pazhankallil enakku ovvoru 'kilo' thaarunkall.

Vendor: **Here you are, your bill is Rs 2,500.**
intharunkall, unkalludaiya 'bill' irandaayiraththi ainuuru ruupaa.

Customer: **Here's three thousand Rupees.**
inthaarum muuvaayiram ruupaa.

Vendor: **Here is the balance of five hundred Rupees.**
inthaarunkall michcham ayinuuru ruupaa.

Customer: **Thank you very much.**
unkallukku mikka nanri.

LESSON 65

Conversation (10) – Making a Doctor's Appointment

Patient: **Hello. This is Stephen. I'd like to make an appointment to see Dr. Ravi.**
hello ithu Stephen. naan Dr. Ravi ai paarka oru 'appointment' vaikka vehnum.

Receptionist: **Certainly. When would you like to see him?**
kaddaayam, eppa avarai paarka virumpukireerka<u>ll</u>?

Patient: **Anytime tomorrow morning would be fine.**
naalaikku-k-kaalai entha nehramum nal-lathu.

Receptionist: **How about 10 AM?**
kaalai paththu mani eppadi?

Patient: **That sounds fine. Thank you.**
athu nal-lathu. nanri.

Receptionist: **We'll see you tomorrow morning, Mr. Stephen.**
naanka<u>ll</u> unka<u>ll</u>ai naalaikku kaalayil kaanpohm, Mr. Stephen.

LESSON 66

Conversation (11) – Seeing the Doctor

Doctor: **Hello Stephen, what can I do for you?**
Hello Stephen, naan unka<u>l</u>ukku enna seiyalaam?

Patient: **Good morning, Dr. Ravi. I have a terrible ache in my lower back.**
kaalai vanakkam Dr. Ravi. enakku kiizh muthuhil sariyaana noh onru irukkirathu.

Doctor: **How long has this been bothering you?**
ithu evvalavu kaalamaaha upaththiravam seyithu?

Patient: **I've been having the pain for about the last 3 weeks.**
noh kadantha muunru kizhamaikalaaka irukkirathu.

Doctor: **Do you have any history of back problems?**
unka<u>l</u>ukku muthuhu pirachchanai munthiyum irunththathaa?

Patient: **No.**
il-lai.

Doctor: **Are you taking any medications at the moment?**
ippohthu ehthaavathu marunthu edukkireerkalaa?

Patient: **No.**
il-lai.

Doctor: **Okay, let's look at your back, this is a muscular pain. Take these painkillers and come and see me in three days.**
sari unka<u>l</u>udaiya muthuhaip paarppohm, ithu 'muscular' noh. intha 'pain killers' ai eduththuviddu muunru naadka<u>l</u>ukkuppin ennai vanthu paarum.

Patient: **OK, doctor. Thank you very much.**
sati 'doctor'. nanri.

Doctor: **And remember not to do any strenuous work that will hurt the back.**
maravaamal muthuhaith thaakkakkuudiya kadinamaana vehlai onrum seyaathehyunka<u>ll</u>.

Patient: **Thank you, Doctor.**
nanri, doctor.

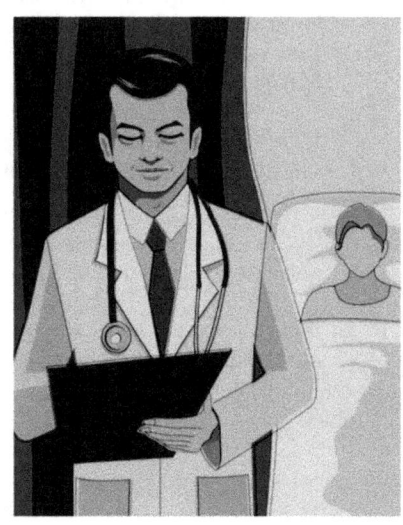

LESSON 67

Conversation (12) – Making Acquaintance

Siva: **Hi, how are you?**
hi, eppadi unka<u>ll</u> sukam?

Mohan: **I am fine, thank you.**
naan nal-la suham, nanri.

Siva: **Are you from around here?**
neenka<u>ll</u> ivvidaththilaa vasikkireerka<u>ll</u>?

Mohan: **Yes, I am from this area, what about you?**
ohm, naan intha idaththai sehnthavar, neenka<u>ll</u> entha idam?

Siva: **I am on holiday here from Brisbane in Australia.**
naan 'Brisbane, Australia'vil irunthu inku vidumuraikku vanthehn.

Mohan: **That's great, have you been to many places?**
athu nal-lathu, pala idankkalukkup pohneenkalaa?

Siva: **Not yet, but I could do with some help.**
innum il-lai, yaarum uthavinaal pohalaam.

Mohan: **I am free on Friday if you need to go sightseeing.**
idankall paarkka pohvathaanaal naan ve<u>lll</u>likizhamai 'free' aaha iruppehn.

Siva: **Oh, that's very good; would you like to join me for lunch today?**
appadiya meththa nallathu; inru mathiya unhavukku ennudan varuveerkalaa?

Mohan: **Yes, most certainly.**
ohm, nichchayamaaha.

Siva:	**Do you know of any good restaurant nearby?** unka<u>ll</u>ukku kiddadiyil u<u>ll</u> <u>ll</u>a nal-la 'restaurant ethuvum theriyumaa?
Mohan:	**Of course, Lucky restaurant is just next door, and they serve very delicious food.** ohmohm, pakkaththil 'Lucky Restaurant' irukkirathu, avarha<u>ll</u>udaiya saappaadu urusiyaanathu.
Siva:	**OK, let's go there.** sari, appa anka pohvohm.
Mohan:	(at the restaurant) **What would you like to eat, buriyani or fried rice?** unka<u>ll</u>ukku enna saappida viruppam, 'buriyani'aa 'fried rice' aa?
Siva:	**I like buriyani.** enaaku 'buriyani' viruppam.
Mohan:	**What drink would you like?** unkallukku kudikka enna viruppam?
Siva:	**I like some orange juice. Thanks.** enakku 'orange juice' viruppam. nanri.
Siva:	**Where do you work?** neenka<u>ll</u> enkeh vehlai seykireerka<u>ll</u>?
Mohan:	**Just across the road, at the Bank.** inthath theruvukku ethiril u<u>ll</u> <u>ll</u>a vankiyil.
Siva:	**At what time have you got to get back?** eththanai manikku thirumpa pohavehnum?
Mohan:	**I have to be there before 2PM.** naan pittpahal irandukku mun nittkavehnum.
Mohan:	**I hope you enjoyed the meal; it was nice meeting you.** saappaaddai rasiththiruppeerka<u>ll</u>, santhiththathil mahizhchi.
Siva:	**Same here.** enakkum mahizhchi.

Mohan: **Here is my telephone number. You can call me when you get home so that we could discuss about going out on Friday.**
ithu enathu 'telephone' ilakkam. veeddukkup pohnapin ennai kooppiddaal ve_ll_ _ll_ikizhamai ve_ll_iyeh pohvathai patty kathaikkalaam.

Siva: **OK, many thanks . See you later.**
sari, mikka nanri. piraku kaanhpohm.

Siva: **Goodbye.**
vanakkam.

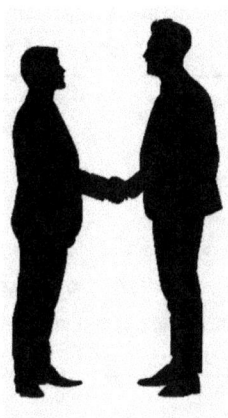

ANSWERS TO EXERCISES

Lesson 3:

மூலை (corner) ; மூளை (brain)

Lesson 4:

Q2.
(i) kulliththehn ; குளித்தேன்
(ii) itukkirathaa ; இருக்கிறதா
(iii) konduvatuhirehn ; கொண்டுவருகிறேன்
(iv) villangkukirathaa ; விளங்குகிறதா
(v) kaathaliththehn ; காதலித்தேன்

Lesson 5:

Q1.
(i) நாளைக்கு எனது பள்ளிக்கூட விடுமுறை முடிகிறது.
(ii) புது வகுப்பில் படிப்பிக்க நல்ல ஆசிரியர்கள் வரவேணும்.
(iii) தமிழ் ஆசிரியர் கெட்டிக்காரனாக இருக்கவேணும்.

Lesson 7:

Q1.
(i) Book ; puththaham ; புத்தகம்
(ii) Friend ; sinehkithan ; சிநேகிதன்
(iii) Brother ; sahotharan ; சகோதரன்
(iv) Duty ; kadamai ; கடமை
(v) Home ; pirappidam / veedu ; பிறப்பிடம் / வீடு
(vi) Brought ; konduvaruthal ; கொண்டுவருதல்
(vii) Will-go ; pohvehn / pohvohm ; போவேன் / போவோம்

LESSON 8:

Q1.

(i) Father ; appah ; தகப்பன்
(ii) Live ; vasi / seevi ; வசி / சீவி
(iii) Temple ; kohvil ; கோவில்
(iv) Name ; peyar ; பெயர்
(v) Occupation ; uththiyoham ; உத்தியோகம்
(vi) Problem ; pirachchanai ; பிரச்சனை
(vii) Time ; nehram ; நேரம்
(viii) Children ; pillaihall ; பிள்ளைகள்
(ix) People ; aadkall /pehr ; ஆட்கள் / பேர்

LESSON 9:

Q1.

(i) Truth ; unmai ; உண்மை
(ii) Baby ; kuzhanthai ; குழந்தை
(iii) Adopt ; thaththedu ; தத்தெடு
(iv) Marriage ; vivaaham ; விவாகம்
(v) Told ; sonnathu ; சொன்னது
(vi) Understand ; vi_ll_ankuthal ; விளங்குதல்

LESSON 10:

Q1.

(i) Shave ; va_ll_i ; வளி
(ii) Haircut ; mudi veddu ; முடி வெட்டு
(iii) Beautiful ; vadivu /azhahu ; வடிவு / அழகு
(iv) Problem ; pirachanai ; பிரச்சனை
(v) Big ; periya ; பெரிய

LESSON 11:

Q1.
(i) Child ; kuzhanthai ; குழந்தை
(ii) Something ; ehthaavathu ; ஏதாவது
(iii) Brush ; thoorikai ; தூரிகை
(iv) Birth – mark ; pirappadaiyaalam ; பிறப்படையாளம்
(v) Long ; neellam ; நீளம்

LESSON 12:

Q1.
(i) Small ; sinna / siriya ; சின்ன / சிறிய
(ii) Bone ; elumpu ; எலும்பு
(iii) Hurt ; thaakku ; தாக்கு
(iv) Take-care ; kavani ; கவனி
(v) Hit ; adi ; அடி
(vi) Swollen ; veenkiyullathu ; வீங்கியுள்ளது

LESSON 13:

Q1.
(i) Infection ; nohyi-th- thotru ; நோய்த் தொற்று
(ii) Pain ; vali/no ; வலி / நோ
(iii) Sore ; punh ; புண்
(iv) Cancer ; putru noi ; புற்று நோய்

LESSON 14:

Q1.
(i) Patient ; noyaali ; நோயாளி
(ii) Stones ; katrkall ; கற்கள்
(iii) Wrong ; pizhai ; பிழை
(iv) Weak ; palaveenam ; பலவீனம்
(v) Operation ; saththira sihichchai ; சத்திர சிகிச்சை

LESSON 14 (continued):

Q2.

(i) அவர் ஒரு இருதய நோயாளி.

(ii) அவருக்கு ஈரலில் புற்று நோய்.

(iii) அவவின் சிறு-நீரகத்தில் கல் இருந்தது.

(iv) உங்களுடைய வயிற்றில் என்ன பிழை? அவருடைய நுரை-ஈரல்கள் பலவீனமாக இருக்கின்றன.

(v) அவவுக்கு உதரத்தில் சத்திரசிகிச்சை நடந்தது.

Q3.
A7; B6; C4; D9; E12; F3; G5; H2; I11; J8; K1; L10

LESSON 15:

Q1.
(i) Keep ; vai ; வை
(ii) Uncomfortable ; asavuhariam ; அசௌஹரியம்
(iii) Closer ; Innum kidda ; இன்னும்கிட்ட
(iv) Bring ; konduvaa ; கொண்டுவா
(v) Bottom ; adippuram ; அடிப்புறம்
(vi) Close ; pooddu ; பூட்டு
(vii) Open ; thira ; திற

Q2.
(i) ஒரு கதிரையில் இரு (ங்கள்).

(ii) மேசைமேல் வை (யுங்கள்).

(iii) இந்தக் கட்டில் எனக்குச் சவுகரியமாக இல்லை.

(iv) இரண்டு எழுத்து மேசைகளையும் கிட்ட வை (யுங்கள்).

(v) அந்தச் சிறு நாற்காலியை இங்கே கொண்டுவா (ருங்கள்).

(vi) அதை அடித்தட்டில் வை (யுங்கள்).

(vii) அந்தக் கதவைப் பூட்டு (ங்கள்).

(viii) யன்னல்களைத் திற (வுங்கள்).

LESSON 16:

Q1.
(i) Hat ; thoppi ; தொப்பி
(ii) Bought ; vaankuthal ; வாங்குதல்
(iii) Colour ; niram ; நிறம்
(iv) Garden ; thohddam ; தோட்டம்
(v) Flower ; puu / malar ; மலர்
(vi) Dog ; naai ; நாய்
(vii) Jumped ; paaithal ; பாய்தல்
(viii) Fence ; vehli ; வேலி

Q2.
(i) நான் ஒரு வெள்ளைத்-தொப்பி வாங்கினேன்.

(ii) கறுப்பு நிறம் அழகானது.

(iii) அவ நீலச் சேலை உடுத்தியிருந்தா.

(iv) தோட்டம் முழுவதும் பச்சையாய் இருந்தது.

(v) அவர் வாகனத்தைச் சிவப்பு 'light'-இல் நிற்பாட்ட வில்லை.

(vi) அது ஒரு வடிவான மஞ்சள் பூ.

(vii) 'brown' நிறமுள்ள நாய் வேலியின் மேல் பாய்ந்தது.

(viii) இளம் சிவப்பு நிறமான உடை அவவுக்கு நல்ல பொருத்தமாய் இருந்தது. எனக்கு ஊதா நிறம் விருப்பம்.

LESSON 17:

Q1.
(i) Sir ; aiaa ; ஐயா
(ii) Brother ; sahotharan ; சகோதரன்
(iii) Hospitality ; upasarippu ; உபசரிப்பு
(iv) Wish ; vaazhthu ; வாழ்த்து
(v) Wedding ; thirumanam ; திருமணம்

LESSON 17 (continued):

Q2.
(i) காலை வணக்கம், ஐயா.
(ii) உங்கள் இரவு நல்லிரவாகுக.
(iii) எப்படி இருக்கிறீர் சகோதகரன்?
(iv) நான் நன்றி கூறுகிறேன்.
(v) உமது உபசரிப்புக்கு மிக்க நன்றி.
(vi) உங்களுக்குப் பிறந்த நாள் வாழ்த்துக்கள்.
(vii) உமக்கு ஆண்டு விழா வாழ்த்துக்கள்.
(viii) உமக்குத் திருமண ஆண்டு விழா வாழ்த்துக்கள்.

LESSON 18:

Q1.
(i) Please ; thayavuseythu ; தயவுசெய்து
(ii) Soon ; kethiyaai ; கெதியாய்
(iii) Home ; veedu ; வீடு
(iv) Short ; kuruhiya / kaddai ; குறுகிய / கட்டை
(v) Route ; vazhi / paathai ; வழி / பாதை
(vi) Fast ; viraivu / thuritham ; விரைவு /துரிதம்
(vii) Fence ; vehli ; வேலி
(viii) Now ; ippohthu ; இப்போது

Q2.
(i) தயவுசெய்து கெதியாய் வாருங்கள்.
(ii) நீ வீட்டுக்குப் போ (நீங்கள் வீட்டுக்குப் போங்கள்).
(iii) குறுக்குவழியை எடுங்கள்.
(iv) விரைவாக நடவுங்கள்.
(v) நான் ஓடப்போகிறேன்.
(vi) வேலி மேலால் பாய் (பாயுங்கள்).
(vii) இங்கே நிறுத்து (ங்கள்).
(viii) இப்போது ஆரம்பி (யுங்கள்).

LESSON 18 (continued):

Q3.
A3; B2; C4; D5; E1

LESSON 19:

Q1.
(i) Go ; poh (nka<u>ll</u>) ; போ (போங்கள்)
(ii) Turn ; thirumpu ; திரும்பு
(iii) Live ; vasi ; வசி
(v) Side ; pakkam ; பக்கம்
(vi) Sun ; sooriyan ; சூரியன்
(vii) Rises ; uthikkirathul/ezhumpukirathu ; உதிக்கிறது/எழும்புகிறது
(viii) Sets ; maraikirathu / amaikkum ; மறைகிறது / அமைக்கும்

Q2.
(i) நேர போ (ங்கள்).
(ii) வலப் பக்கம் திரும்பு (ங்கள்).
(iii) இடப் பக்கம் திரும்பு (ங்கள்).
(iv) மேலே போ (ங்கள்).
(v) கிழே போ(ங்கள்).
(vi) நாங்கள் தெற்குப் பக்கத்தில் வசிக்கிறோம்.
(vii) யாழ்ப்பாணம் இலங்கையின் வடப்பக்கத்தில் இருக்கிறது.
(viii) சூரியன் கிழக்கில் உதிக்கிறது.
(ix) சூரியன் மேற்கில் மறைகிறது.

LESSON 20:

Q1.
(i) Occupation ; uththiyohkam ; உத்தியோகம்
(ii) How-many ; eththanai ; எத்தனை
(iii) Older ; muuththa ; மூத்த
(iv) Younger ; i<u>ll</u>aiya ; இளைய

LESSON 20 (continued):

Q2.
(i) உங்களுடைய தகப்பனின் (அப்பாவின்) உத்தியோகம் என்ன?

(ii) உங்களுடைய தாய் (அம்மா) எங்கே?

(iii) இவர் உங்களுடைய மகனா?

(iv) உங்களுக்கு எத்தனை மகள்மார்?

(v) உங்களுடைய அக்காவுக்கு எத்தனை வயது?

(vi) உங்களுடைய தங்கை என்ன செய்கிறா?

(vii) அவர் உங்களுடைய அண்ணனா?

(viii) உங்களுக்கு எத்தனை தம்பிமார்?

LESSON 21:

Q1.
(i) Work ; vehlai ; வேலை
(ii) Here ; inkeh ; இங்கே
(iii) Nice ; nal-la / arumaiyaana ; நல்ல / அருமையான
(iv) Live ; vasi ; வசி

Q2.
(i) யார் உங்களுடைய மாமா?

(ii) உங்களுடைய மாமி எங்கே வசிக்கிறா?

(iii) உங்களுடைய மைத்துணி எங்கே வேலை செய்கிறா?

(iv) உங்களுடைய மைத்துணன் ஒரு நல்லவர் போல் தெரிகிறார்.

(v) உங்களுடைய தாத்தா இங்கே இருக்கிறாரா?

(vi) உங்களுடைய பாட்டி உம்முடனா வசிக்கிறா?

LESSON 22:

Q1.
(i) Came ; vanthathu ; வந்தது
(ii) United ; ottrumaiyaana ; ஒற்றுமையான
(iii) Died ; iraththal / mariththal ; இறத்தல் / மரித்தல்
(iv) Beautiful ; vadivaana / azhahaana ; வடிவான / அழகான
(v) Loves ; anpu ko<u>ll</u> <u>ll</u>uthal ; அன்புகொள்ளுதல்
(vi) Lot ; athika / niraya ; அதிக / நிறைய

Q2.
(i) 'ராமா' அவவுடைய புருஷன்.
(ii) 'பாலன்' தன்னுடைய மனைவியுடன் வந்தார்.
(iii) அவர்கள் ஒரு ஒற்றுமையான குடும்பம்.
(iv) அவருடைய மாமனார் இங்கு வசிக்கிறார்.
(v) அவவுடைய மாமியார் போன வருஷம் இறந்துபோனா.
(vi) சின்னராசாவுக்கு வடிவான இரண்டு பேத்திமார் இருக்கிறார்கள்.
(vii) ரமேசுக்கு அவர் பேரனில் அதிக அன்பு.

LESSON 23:

Q1.
(i) Going ; purappaduthal / pohkuthal
(ii) Another ; innoru
(iii) Need ; thehvai / avasiyam
(iv) Give ; thaa (runka<u>ll</u>)
(v) Will-write ; ezhuthuvehn / ezhuthuvohm

Q2.
(i) நான் தபால் கந்தோருக்குப் போகிறேன்.
(ii) நான் இன்னொரு கடிதம் அவசியம் எழுத வேணும்.
(iii) தயவு செய்து இந்த பார்சலை போஸ்ற் பண்ணுவீரா?
(iv) தயவுசெய்து எனக்கு மூன்று ஐம்பது ரூபா முத்திரைகள் தாருங்கள்.
(v) தயவுசெய்து ஒரு ரெஜிஸ்ரெட் கடிதத்துக்கு முத்திரைகள் தாருங்கள்.
(vi) நான் முகவரியைக் கடித உறையில் எழுதுவேன்.

LESSON 24:

Q1.
(i) Caught ; ahappaduthal
(ii) Beyond ; appaal
(iii) Look ; paar
(iv) Going ; purappaduthal / pohkuthal

Q2.
(i) உள்ளே போ (ங்கள்).
(ii) வெளியே வா (ருங்கள்).
(iii) நீங்கள் இடையே அகப்பட்டு விட்டீர்கள்.
(iv) அது கதவுக்கு அப்பாலே.
(v) கீழ் மாடியில் போய்ப் பார் (பாருங்கள்).
(vi) நான் மேல்மாடிக்குப் போகிறேன்.
(vii) நாங்கள் கீழ் மாடிக்குப் போகவேணும்.

LESSON 25:

Q1.
(i) Nation ; thehsam ; தேசம்
(ii) Heart ; ithayam / iruthayam ; இதயம் / இருதயம்
(iii) Corner ; muulai ; மூலை
(iv) Medals ; pathakkanka<u>ll</u> ; பதக்கங்கள்
(v) Sides ; pakkanka<u>ll</u> ; பக்கங்கள்
(vi) Lucky-number ; athirsda ilakkam ; அதிர்ஷ்ட இலக்கம்
(vii) Church ; thehvaalayam / kohvil ; தேவாலயம் / கோவில்
(viii) Planet ; kiraham ; கிரகம்
(ix) Commandments ; katrpanaiha<u>ll</u> ; கற்பனைகள்

LESSON 25 (continued):

Q2.
(i) ஒரு நாடு ஒரு தேசம்.
(ii) இரு இதயங்கள் இணைந்தன.
(iii) ஒரு சதுரத்துக்கு நாலு மூலைகள்.
(iv) 'மோகன்' ஐந்து பதக்கங்களை வென்றார்.
(v) தாயக் கட்டைக்கு ஆறு பக்கங்கள்.
(vi) ஏழு ஒரு அதிர்ஷ்ட இலக்கமா?
(vii) இந்த நகரத்தில் எட்டுக் கோவில்கள் இருக்கின்றன.
(viii) ஒன்பது கிரகங்கள் மனிதரைத் தாக்குகின்றன.
(ix) கடவுளின் பத்துக் கற்பனைகளை அனுசரிக்கவும்.

LESSON 26:

Q1.
(i) Less ; kuraivu ; குறைவு
(ii) Greater ; periyathu ; பெரியது
(iii) Odd ; ottrai ; ஒற்றை
(iv) Even ; iraddai ; இரட்டை

Q2.
(i) பத்தும் ஒன்றும் பதினொன்று.
(ii) பதினைந்தில் ஐந்து குறைந்தால் பத்து.
(iii) பன்னிரண்டு பதினாலிலும் சிறியது.
(iv) பதினாறு பதின்மூன்றிலும் பெரியது.
(v) பதினேழு ஒரு ஒற்றை இலக்கம்.
(vi) பத்து ஒரு இரட்டை இலக்கம்.
(vii) பன்னிரண்டு பொருட்கள் ஒரு 'டஸின்' எனப்படும்.

LESSON 27:

Q1.
(i) Times ; tharam / murai ; தரம் / முறை
(ii) Means ; enraal / vasathi ; என்றால் / வசதி
(iii) Century ; nuuru ; நூறு
(iv) But ; aanaal ; ஆனால்

Q2.
(i) பத்தும் பத்தும் இருபது.
(ii) இரண்டு தரம் இருபது நாற்பது.
(iii) எண்பதில் இருந்து முப்பது போனால் ஐம்பது.
(iv) ஐந்து, நூறுக்குள் இருபது தரம் போகும்.
(v) நூறு என்றால் ஒரு 'செஞ்சரி'.
(vi) முப்பத்தி ஆறும் நாற்பத்தி இரண்டும் எவ்வளவு?
(vii) ஏழு தரம் ஏழு அல்ல, ஆனால் ஏழு தரம் எழுபது.

LESSON 29:

Q1.
(i) Percent ; veetham ; வீதம்
(ii) Runs ; ohddankall ; ஓட்டங்கள்
(iii) Old ; pazhaiya/vayathupohna ; பழைய /வயதுபோன
(iv) Ago ; munpu ; முன்பு
(v) Students ; maanavarha<u>ll</u> ; மாணவர்கள்
(vi) Sold ; vilaippaddathu ; விலைப்பட்டது
(vii) Collection ; vasool ; வசூல்
(viii) Nearly ; kiddaththadda ; கிட்டத்தட்ட
(ix) Talking ; kathaippathu ; கதைப்பது

LESSON 29 (continued):

Q2.
(i) நூற்றி ஐம்பது வீதம்.
(ii) இருநூற்றி இருபது ஓட்டங்கள்.
(iii) இருநூறு வருடங்கள் பழையன.
(iv) நானூறு வருடங்களுக்கு முன்பு.
(v) அறுநூறு மாணவர்கள் இருக்கிறார்கள்.
(vi) எழுநூறு நுழைவுச் சீட்டுகள் விலைப்பட்டன.
(vii) வசூல் கிட்டத்தட்ட ஆயிரம் 'டாலர்ஸ்' மட்டில் வந்தது.
(viii) நாங்கள் ஆயிரத்தில் கதைக்கிறோம்.

LESSON 30:

Q1.
(i) Many ; pala ; பல
(ii) More ; mehlaaha / athiham ; மேலாக / அதிகம்
(iii) Live ; vasi ; வசி
(iv) Countries ; naaduhall ; நாடுகள்

LESSON 31:

Q1.
(i) Children ; pill llaihall ; பிள்ளைகள்
(ii) Born ; piranthathu ; பிறந்தது
(iii) Family ; kudumpam ; குடும்பம்
(iv) Arrive ; varuhai ; வருகை
(v) Receives ; peruthal / kidaiththal ; பெறுதல் / கிடைத்தல்
(vi) Race ; ohddappanthayam ; ஓட்டப்பந்தயம்
(vii) Agenda ; seyal thiddam ; செயல் திட்டம்

LESSON 31 (continued):

Q2.
(i) ஐந்து பிள்ளைகளில் முதல் மூன்றும் ஆண்கள்.
(ii) எனது குடும்பத்தில் நான் நாலாவதாகப் பிறந்தேன்.
(iii) 'சிவா' ஐந்தாவதாக வருகை தந்தார்.
(iv) மூன்றாவது இடத்துக்கு வெண்கலப் பதக்கம் கிடைக்கிறது.
(v) சுந்தர் ஓட்டப் பந்தயத்தில் இரண்டாவதாக வந்தார்.
(vi) அவர் வகுப்பில் முதலாவதாக வந்தார்.
(vii) செயல் திட்டத்தில் ஏழாவதாக என்ன இருக்கிது?

LESSON 32:

Q1.
(i) Now ; ippa / ippohthu ; இப்ப / இப்போது
(ii) Show ; kaaddu / kaadchi ; காட்டு / காட்சி
(iii) Start ; aarampi / thodanku ; ஆரம்பி / தொடங்கு
(iv) Coming ; varuthal ; வருதல்
(v) Always ; eppohthum / eppavum ; எப்போதும் / எப்பவும்
(vi) Match ; poruththu / pohddy ; பொருத்து / போட்டி
(vii) Better ; sitantha / nal-lathu ; சிறந்த / நல்லது
(viii) Early ; ve<u>ll</u> <u>l</u>ana ; வெள்ளன
(ix) Watch ; kaaval / kadikaaram ; காவல் / கைக்கடிகாரம்
(x) Fast ; vehkamaaha ; வேகமாக

LESSON 33:

Q1.
(i) Today ; inraikku / inru ; இன்றைக்கு / இன்று
(ii) Meeting ; santhiththal / kuuddam ; சந்தித்தல் / கூட்டம்
(iii) Tomorrow ; naa<u>l</u>laikku / naa<u>ll</u>ai ; நாளைக்கு / நாளை
(iv) Answer ; marrumozhi / vidai / pathil ; மறுமொழி / விடை / பதில்
(v) Hide ; marai / o<u>ll</u>i ; மறை / ஒளி
(vi) Careful ; kavanam / paththiram ; கவனம் / பத்திரம்
(vii) Thought ; yohsanai / ennam ; யோசனை / எண்ணம்
(viii) Wrong ; thappu / pizhai ; தப்பு / பிழை

LESSON 34:

Q1.
(i) Rains ; mazhai peythal ; மழை பெய்தல்
(ii) Busy ; ohivil-laatha ; ஓய்வில்லாத
(iii) Overseas ; ve<u>ll</u>inaadu ; வெளிநாடு
(iv) Birthday ; pirantha naall ; பிறந்த நாள்
(v) Cold ; ku<u>l</u>ir ; குளிர்
(vi) Anniversary ; aandu vizhaa ; ஆண்டு விழா
(vii) Mid ; nadu / naduppahuthi ; நடு / நடுப்பகுதி

Q2.
பள்ளிக்கூட கிறிஸ்மஸ் விடுமுறை இங்கு கார்த்திகைக் கடைசி வாரத்தில் தொடங்கும்.

LESSON 35:

Q1.
(i) Holiday ; vidumurai ; விடுமுறை
(ii) Someone ; yaaroh ; யாரோ
(iii) Night ; iravu ; இரவு
(iv) Flight ; vimaana-p-payanham ; விமானப் பயணம்
(v) Lunch ; mathiya saappaadu ; மதிய சாப்பாடு
(vi) Next ; aduththa ; அடுத்த
(vii) Visitors ; virunththaa<u>ll</u>iha<u>ll</u> ; விருந்தாளிகள்

LESSON 36:

Q1.
(i) Works ; vehlai seythal ; வேலை செய்தல்
(ii) Appointment ; sa<u>n</u>thippu munpathivu ; சந்திப்பு முன்பதிவு
(iii) Consult ; aalohsi ; ஆலோசி
(iv) Hospital ; aaspaththiri ; ஆஸ்பத்திரி
(v) Brilliant ; sirappu vai<u>n</u>tha/thirammikka ; சிறப்பு வாய்ந்த / திறமிக்க
(vi) Yesterday ; nehtru ; நேற்று

LESSON 36 (continued):
Q2.
(i) அவர் ஒரு நல்ல ஆசிரியர்.
(ii) நான் ஒரு அர்ச்சகரைக் காணவேணும்.
(iii) 'ரமணா' ஒரு பொறியியலாளராக வேலை செய்கிறார்.
(iv) எனக்கு வைத்தியருடன் ஒரு சந்திப்பு முன்பதிவு ('appointment') இருக்குது.
(v) நான் ஒரு வழக்கறிஞருடன் ஆலோசிக்கவேணும்.
(vi) 'மாலா' ஆஸ்பத்திரியில் தலைமைத் தாதி.
(vii) 'ஜான்' ஒரு வெறும் குமாஸ்தா.
(viii) 'சுரேசன்' ஒரு சிறப்பு வாய்ந்த கணக்காளர்.
(ix) 'கோபி' யை போலீஸ்காரர் நேற்றுக் கைது செய்தார்கள்.

LESSON 37:
Q1.
(i) Stop ; niruththu / nitrpaaddu ; நிறுத்து / நிற்பாட்டு
(ii) Freedom ; suthanthiram ; சுதந்திரம்
(iii) Poisonous ; vishamaanathu ; விஷமானது
(iv) Snake ; paampu ; பாம்பு
(v) Plan ; thiddam ; திட்டம்
(vi) President ; janaathipathi ; ஜனாதிபதி

LESSON 38:
Q1.
(i) Long time ; pala kaalam ; பல காலம்
(ii) Adore ; mikka nehsam koll ; மிக்க நேசம் கொள்
(iii) Laid ; iddathu / vaippathu ; இட்டது / வைப்பது
(iv) Eggs ; muddai ; முட்டை
(v) Lot ; kanakka / pakuthi ; கனக்க / பகுதி
(vi) Please ; thayavu seythu ; தயவு செய்து
(vii) Apply ; puusu / pohdu ; பூசு / போடு
(viii) Torturing ; siththiravathai seythal ; சித்திரவதை செய்தல்
(ix) Pet ; sellappiraanhi ; செல்லப்பிராணி
(x) Favourite ; mihappiriyamaana ; மிகப்பிரியமான

LESSON 39:

Q1.
(i) Mother ; ammaa ; அம்மா
(ii) Every ; ovvoru ; ஒவ்வொரு
(iii) Cart ; vanhdil ; வண்டில்
(iv) Pull ; izhu ; இழு
(v) Tasty ; urusaiyaana / suvaiyaana ; உருசையான / சுவையான
(vi) Filthy ; uuththai ; ஊத்தை
(vii) Road ; theru ; தெரு
(viii) House ; veedu ; வீடு
(ix) Forest ; kaadu / vanam ; காடு / வனம்
(x) Bathe ; ku<u>ll</u>i ; குளி
(xi) Zoo ; miruhakkaadchich saalai ; மிருகக்காட்சிச் சாலை

LESSON 40:

Q1.
(i) Garden ; thohddam ; தோட்டம்
(ii) Webs ; valaiha<u>ll</u> ; வலைகள்
(iii) Wall ; suvar ; சுவர்
(iv) Pond ; ku<u>ll</u>am ; குளம்
(v) Everywhere ; el laa idamum/enkum ; எல்லா இடமும் / எங்கும்
(vi) Jungle ; kaadu / kurunkaadu ; காடு / குறுங்காடு

LESSON 41:

Q1.
(i) Get me ; eduththuththaa (runka<u>ll</u>) ; எடுத்துத்தா (ருங்கள்)
(ii) Keep ; vai (unka<u>ll</u>) ; வை (யுங்கள்)
(iii) Give me ; thaa (runka<u>ll</u>) ; தா (ருங்கள்)
(iv) Food ; saappaadu / unhavu ; சாப்பாடு / உணவு
(v) Will-eat ; saappiduvehn (saappiduvohm) ; (சாப்பிடுவோம்)

LESSON 42:

Q1.
(i) Taste ; suvai / utusi-paar ; சுவை / உருசி பார்
(ii) Favourite ; mihappiriyamaana ; மிகப்பிரியமான
(iii) Vegetables ; kaai kari (matakkari) ; காய் கறி / மரக்கறி
(iv) Heart ; iruthayam / ithayam ; இருதயம் / இதயம்
(v) Cooking ; samaiyal ; சமையல்
(vi) Need ; thehvai / avasiyam ; தேவை / அவசியம்
(vii) Here ; inkeh ; இங்கே
(viii) Readily ; ilahuvaaka / chulapamaaka ; இலகுவாக / சுலபமாக

LESSON 43:

Q1.
(i) Buy ; vaanku ; வாங்கு
(ii) Expensive ; athika vilai/sariyaana vilai ; அதிக விலை / சரியான விலை
(iii) Health ; sukam / aarohkkiam ; சுகம் / ஆரோக்கியம்
(iv) Fruits ; pazhankall ; பழங்கள்
(v) Season ; patuva kalam ; பருவ காலம்
(vi) Milk ; paal ; பால்

LESSON 44:

Q1.
(i) Generally ; pothuvaaha ; பொதுவாக
(ii) Most-people ; anehamaanavarkal ; அநேகமானவர்கள்
(iii) Both ; itandum / ituvarum ; இரண்டும் / இருவரும்
(iv) Exports ; ehttrumathikall ; ஏற்றுமதிகள்
(v) Tastier ; mikka urusai ; மிக்க உருசை

LESSON 45:

Q1.
(i) Preparation ; thayaarippu ; தயாரிப்பு
(ii) Delicious ; insuvai mihunthathu ; இன்சுவை மிகுந்தது
(iii) Prefer ; kuuda viruppam ; கூட விருப்பம்
(iv) Friend ; nanhpan / sinehkithan ; நண்பன் / சிநேகிதன்
(v) Eat ; saappidu ; சாப்பிடு
(vi) Cooks ; samaiyalkaararka<u>ll</u> ; சமையல்காரர்கள்

Q2.
(i) இந்த மாட்டிறைச்சி தயாரிப்பு நல்ல உருசி.
(ii) நான் குட்டி ஆட்டு இறைச்சியை விட, ஆட்டிறைச்சியை கூட விரும்புகிறேன்.
(iii) என்னுடைய நண்பன் மாட்டிறைச்சி சாப்பிடமாட்டார்.
(iv) பன்றி இறைச்சியைப் பலபேர் சாப்பிடுவதில்லை.
(v) என்னுடைய அம்மா நல்ல உருசையான கோழி இறைச்சிக் கறி சமைப்பா.
(vi) இன்று நாங்கள் கொஞ்ச 'சிக்கன் நகெற்ஸ்' வாங்குவோம்

LESSON 46:

Q1.
(i) Borrow ; kadan vaanku ; கடன் வாங்கு
(ii) Give-me ; thaa (runka<u>ll</u>) ; தா (ருங்ககள்)
(iii) Need ; thehvai / avasiyam ; தேவை / அவசியம்
(iv) Paper ; kadathaasi ; கடதாசி
(v) Get-yourself ; petrtukko<u>ll</u> (<u>ll</u> unka<u>ll</u>) ; பெற்றுக்கொள்.
                                                            (ளுங்கள்)

Q2.
(i) நான் உங்களுடைய பேனையைக் கொஞ்ச நேரம் கடன் வாங்கலாமா?
(ii) எனக்கு ஒரு இறப்பர் <u>தாரும்</u> எங்களுக்கு ஒரு 'ஸ்டப்லேர்' அல்லது ஒரு கடதாசி 'கிளிப்' <u>தேவை</u>.
(iii) உங்களுக்கு ஒரு அடிமட்டம் தேவைப்படும்.
(iv) நீங்கள் ஒரு 'பென்சில் ஷார்ப்பேனரை' பெற்றுக்கொள்ளவேணும்.

LESSON 47:

Q1.
(i) Bought ; vaankinehn/vaankinohm ; வாங்கினேன்/ வாங்கினோம்
(ii) Received ; kidaiththathu ; கிடைத்தது
(iii) Transaction ; kodukkal vaankal ; கொடுக்கல்-வாங்கல்
(iv) Big ; peria ; பெரிய

Q2.
(i) நான் இதை நல்ல மலிவாக வாங்கினேன்.
(ii) எனக்கு நல்ல விலை தள்ளுபடி கிடைத்தது.
(iii) இந்தக் கொடுக்கல் வாங்கலுக்கு 'புரோக்கர் கொமிசன்' மிக்க அதிகம்.
(iv) நான் அந்தத் தர்மத்துக்கு பெரிய நன்கொடை செய்தேன்.

LESSON 48:

Q1.
(i) Studied ; padiththehn ; படித்தேன்
(ii) Many ; pala ; பல
(iii) Far ; thuuram ; தூரம்
(iv) Churches ; thehvaalayankall / kohvilkall ; தேவாலயங்கள் / கோவில்கள்
(v) Lecturer ; virivuraiaalar ; விரிவுரையாளர்
(vi) Very big ; mikapperiya ; மிகப்பெரிய

Q2.
(i) நான் இரண்டு கல்லூரிகளில் படித்தேன்.
(ii) நான் இங்கு பல 'ப்ரொட்டஸ்டன்ட்' தேவாலயங்களைப் பார்க்கிறேன்.
(iii) உம்முடைய வீட்டுக்குக்கிட்ட உள்ள ஆஸ்பத்திரி எவ்வளவு தூரம்?
(iv) இவ்விடத்தில் கத்தோலிக்க தேவாலயங்கள் இருக்கிறதா?
(v) 'கௌரி' கொழும்புப் பல்கலைக்கழகத்தில் ஒரு விரிவுரையாளர்.
(vi) எங்களிடம் ஒரு மிகப்பெரிய விமான நிலையம் இருக்கிறது.

LESSON 49:

Q1.
(i) Last - week ; pohna kizhamai ; போன கிழமை
(ii) From-here ; inkirunthu ; இங்கிருந்து
(iii) Arriving ; vatukiraar / vatukirathu ; வருகிறார் / வருகிறது
(iv) Enjoyed ; inpamadainththehn ; இன்பமடைந்ததேன்

Q2.
(i) நான் போன கிழமை ஒரு புதுக் 'கார்' வாங்கினேன்.
(ii) இங்கிருந்து கொழும்புக்கு ஒரு 'பஸ்' இருக்குதா?
(iii) என்னுடைய சகோதரர் இன்று விமானத்தால் வருகிறார்.
(iv) நேற்று நான் 'ஹெலிகாப்டர் ' சவாரியை அனுபவித்தேன்.

LESSON 50:

Q1.
(i) Small ; siru / sinna ; சிறு / சின்ன
(ii) Activity ; seyal ; செயல்
(iii) Peaceful ; samaathaanamaana ; சமாதானமான
(iv) Culture ; kalaachchaaram ; கலாச்சாரம்
(v) Work ; vehlai ; வேலை

Q2.
(i) நான் ஒரு சிறு நகரத்தில் வளர்ந்தேன்.
(ii) மா நகரத்தில் இரவுகளில் பல கேளிக்கைச் சம்பவங்கள் இருக்கின்றன.
(iii) எங்களுடைய நாடு ஓரளவு சமாதானமானது.
(iv) கிராமிய மக்களுக்கு ஒரு தனி கலாச்சாரம் இருக்கிறது.
(v) அதிகமான ஆட்கள் நகரம் சார்ந்த இடங்களில் வேலை செய்ய விரும்புவர்.

LESSON 51:

Q1.
(i) Front ; munpakkam ; முன்பக்கம்
(ii) Near ; atukil / kidda ; அருகில் / கிட்ட
(iii) Very-nice ; arumaiyaana ; அருமையான
(iv) Garden ; thohddam ; தோட்டம்
(v) Weed-killer ; ka<u>ll</u>ai naasini ; களை நாசினி
(vi) Wife ; manaivi ; மனைவி

Q2.
(i) உங்களிடம் முன்னுக்கு அழகான தோட்டம் இருக்கிறது.
(ii) பொது பூங்காவனம் ஒன்று எங்கள் வீட்டுக்கு அருகில் உள்ளது.
(iii) அந்த புல் பார்வைக்கு அருமையாக இருக்கிறது.
(iv) உங்களுடைய தோட்டத்தில் பல செடிகள் இருக்கின்றன.
(v) நான் என்னுடைய செடிகளுக்கு களைநாசினி தெளிக்க வேணும்.
(vi) நான் என்னுடைய மனைவிக்கு கொஞ்ச பூ வாங்க வேணும்.

LESSON 52:

Q1.
(i) Health ; udal nalam/aatohkkiam ; உடல் நலம் / ஆரோக்கியம்
(ii) Essential ; aththiyaavasiyam ; அத்தியாவசியம்
(iii) Most ; anehkamaana ; அநேகமான
(iv) Used ; paaviththa ; பாவித்த
(v) Flavour ; vaasanai ; வாசனை

Q2.
(i) அதிக மஞ்சள் உடல் நலத்துக்கு நல்லதல்ல.
(ii) இஞ்சி ஆசிய சமையலுக்கு அத்தியாவசியமான செய்பொருள்.
(iii) அநேகமான இந்தியன் கறிகளுக்கு மிளகாய்த் தூள் பாவிக்கப்படுகிறது.
(iv) கறித் தூளை மிளகாய்த் தூளுடன் கலந்து பாவிக்கலாம்.
(v) கறிகளுக்கு வாசனை தர கறுவா பாவிக்கப்படுகிறது.

LESSON 53:

Q1.
(i) Happy ; makizhchiyaana ; மகிழ்ச்சியான
(ii) Government ; atasaankam ; அரசாங்கம்
(iii) Family ; kudumpam ; குடும்பம்
(iv) Freedom ; suthanthiram ; சுதந்திரம்
(v) Stress ; manavulaichchal ; மனவுளைச்சல்

Q2.
(i) மக்கள் தற்கால அரசாங்கத்துடன் மகிழ்ச்சியாக இருக்கிறார்கள்.
(ii) ஆண் ஒரு குடும்பத்தின் தலைவன்.
(iii) இந்த நாட்களில் பிள்ளைகளுக்கு அதிகமான சுதந்திரம் இருக்கிறது.
(iv) பல்கலைக்கழக மாணவர்களுக்கு நிறைய மனவுளைச்சல்.

LESSON 54:

Q1.
(i) Library ; noolakam ; நூலகம்
(ii) Documents ; aava-nhankall ; ஆவணங்கள்
(iii) Unattended ; kavanikkappadaatha ; கவனிக்கப்படாத
(iv) Arrange ; ozhunkupaduththu ; ஒழுங்குபடுத்து
(v) Move ; nakarththu ; நகர்த்து
(vi) Files ; kohppukall ; கோப்புகள்

Q2.
(i) நான் அந்த புத்தகத்தை நூலகத்தில் இரவல் வாங்கினேன்.
(ii) அந்த ஆவணங்களைக் கூடையில் போடவும்.
(iii) அந்தத்தட்டில் ஒரு தொகை கவனிக்கப்படாத கடிதங்கள் இருக்கின்றன.
(iv) என்னுடைய புத்த நிலைப் பெட்டியை சரியான முறையில் ஒழுங்குபடுத்த வேணும்.
(v) நாங்கள் நிலைப்பெட்டியை மற்ற மூலைக்கு நகர்த்துவோம்.
(vi) தயவு செய்து சம்பந்தப்பட்ட கோப்புகளைத் திறக்கவும்.

LESSON 55:

Q1.
(i) Speak ; kathai ; கதை
(ii) Catching ; pidiththal ; பிடித்தல்
(iii) Little ; koncham ; கொஞ்சம்
(iv) Road ; theru / paathai ; தெரு / பாதை

Q2.
(i) நீங்கள் சரியான துரிதமாகக் கதைக்கிறீர்கள்.

(ii) அவர்கள் மெதுவாக எங்களைப் பிடிக்கிறார்கள்.

(iii) இன்னும் கொஞ்சம் விரைவாக ஓட்டும்.

(iv) இந்தத் தெருவில் வேகமூட்டுதல் இயலாது.

ADDITIONAL VOCABULARY

A

accident	vipaththu	விபத்து
across	marupakkam	மறுபக்கம்
adult	vayathuvantha	வயது வந்த
after	pirahu	பிறகு
again	meendum	மீண்டும்
agree	inhangu	இணங்கு
air	kaatru	காற்று
all	ella	எல்லா
alone	thaniya	தனிய
among	idaiye	இடையே
amount	thohai	தொகை
angel	thehvathuuthar	தேவதூதர்
animal	miruham	மிருகம்
answer	vidai	விடை

B

baby	-	kuzhanthai	-	குழந்தை
bad	-	kedda	-	கெட்ட
bag	-	pai	-	பை
bangle	-	valaiyal	-	வளையல்
bat	-	vawvaal	-	வெளவால்
beach	-	kadatkarai	-	கடற்கரை
beat	-	adi	-	அடி
belt	-	paddi	-	பட்டி
beauty	-	azhahu	-	அழகு
before	-	munpu	-	முன்பு
blood	-	iraththam	-	இரத்தம்
body	-	udampu	-	உடம்பு
boil	-	kothikkavai	-	கொதிக்கவை
bread	-	paan	-	பாண்
		roddy	-	ரொட்டி
breakfast	-kaalaichchaappaadu	-	காலைச்சாப்பாடு

C

cap	-	thoppi	-	தொப்பி
clap	-	kaithaddu	-	கைதட்டு
clean	-	thupparavu	-	துப்பரவு
cloth	-	thunhi	-	துணி
coffee	-	kohppi	-	கோப்பி
	-	kaappi		காப்பி
colour	-	niram	-	நிறம்

comb	-	seeppu	-	சீப்பு
common	-	pothu	-	பொது
count	-	ennhu	-	எண்ணு
cross	-	kurusu / siluvai	-	குருசு/சிலுவை
cruel	-	irakkamatra	-	இரக்கமற்ற
		kodiya	-	கொடிய

D

darkness	-	iruddu	-	இருட்டு
deaf	-	sevidu	-	செவிடு
delay	-	thaamathi	-	தாமதி
desire	-	aarvam	-	ஆர்வம்
devil	-	saaththaan	-	சாத்தான்
dinner	-	iravuchchaappadu	-	இரவுச்சாப்பாடு
dirty	-	asuththam	-	அசுத்தம்
disease	-	nohyi	-	நோய்
doubt	-	aimichcham	-	ஐமிச்சம்
	-	sanththeham	-	சந்தேகம்
dream	-	kanavu	-	கனவு
dress	-	udai /	-	உடை /
		uduththu	-	உடுத்து

E

eat	-	saappidu	-	சாப்பிடு
earlier	-	munpu	-	முன்பு
end	-	mudivu	-	முடிவு
enjoy	-	anupavi	-	அனுபவி

entrance	-	nuzhaivaayil	-	நுழைவாயில்	
erase	-	azhi	-	அழி	
escape	-	thappippoh	-	தப்பிப்போ	
exit	-	velliyehru	-	வெளியேறு	

F

face	-	muham	-	முகம்
fail	-	thohttruppoh	-	தோற்றுப்போ
faint	-	mayakkamadai	-	மயக்கமடை
fan	-	visiri	-	விசிறி
farm	-	pannhai	-	பண்ணை
fat	-	kozhuppu	-	கொழுப்பு
feel	-	unhar	-	உணர்
fence	-	vehli	-	வேலி
festival	-	thiruvizhaa	-	திருவிழா
fever	-	kaaichchal	-	காய்ச்சல்
fill	-	nirappu	-	நிரப்பு
fog	-	muudupani	-	மூடுபனி
fool	-	madaiyan	-	மடையன்
foolish	-	madaiththanam	-	மடைத்தனம்
full	-	nirampiya / niraiya	-	நிரம்பிய / நிறைய

G

gate	-	nuzhaivazhi	-	நுழைவழி
	-	nuzhaivaasal	-	நுழைவாசல்

gem	-	iraththinakkal	-	இரத்தினக்கல்
general	-	pothu	-	பொது
giddiness	-	thalaichchutru	-	தலைச்சுற்று
gift	-	anapa<u>l</u>ippu	-	அன்பளிப்பு
god	-	kadavul	-	கடவுள்
gold	-	thankam	-	தங்கம்
government	-	arasaankam	-	அரசாங்கம்
gravel	-	saralaikkal	-	சரளைக்கல்
gravy	-	kuzhampu	-	குழம்பு
ground	-	tharai	-	தரை
gun	-	thuppaakki	-	துப்பாக்கி

H

health	-	savukkiam	-	சவுக்கியம்
heaven	-	suvarkkam	-	சுவர்க்கம்
heavy	-	paaramaana	-	பாரமான
hell	-	naraham	-	நரகம்
hill	-	kunru / malai	-	குன்று / மலை
honest	-	nehrmaiyaana	-	நேர்மையான
hopper	-	aappam	-	அப்பம்
hot	-	suudaana / veppamaana	-	சூடான / வெப்பமான

I

imagination	-	katpanai	-	கற்பனை

innocent	-	kallankam il-laatha / appaavi	- களங்கமில்லாத/ அப்பாவி
itch	-	arippu / sorri	- அரிப்பு / சொறி
insult	-	avamathi / ninthi	- அவமதி / நிந்தி

J

jaggery	-	sakkarai / vel-lam	- சக்கரை / வெல்லம்
jam	-	jam	- பழத்துவை
joint	-	muuddu	- மூட்டு
joke	-	pahudi / nahaichchuvai	- பகுடி / நகைச்சுவை

K

king	-	raja	- அரசன்
kiss	-	muththam	- முத்தம்
kitchen	-	samayalarai / kusini	- சமையலறை / குசினி
know	-	arrinthukoll	- அறிந்துகொள்

L

lake	-	ehri	- ஏரி
lame	-	mudavan	- முடவன்
lick	-	nakku	- நக்கு

lie -	poi -	பொய்
lift -	uyarththu / thookku -	உயர்த்து / தூக்கு
light -	ve<u>ll</u>ichcham -	வெளிச்சம்
lightening -	minnal -	மின்னல்
liquor -	mathupaanam -	மதுபானம்
listen -	keh<u>ll</u> -	கேள்
load -	paaram / sumai -	பாரம் / சுமை
lock -	puuddu -	பூட்டு
lose -	izha / tholai -	இழ / தொலை
loss -	naddam -	நட்டம்
lost -	izhantha -	இழந்த
love -	anpu / kaathal -	அன்பு / காதல்
luggage -	payanhappeddi -	பயணப்பெட்டி

M

matchbox -	thiip-peddi -	தீப்பெட்டி
magazine -	sanjikai -	சஞ்சிகை
meal -	unhavu -	உணவு
memory -	gnaapaham -	ஞாபகம்
method -	seyalmurai -	செயல்முறை
milk -	paal -	பால்
mind -	manam -	மனம்

minute	-	nimidam / mikachchiriya	நிமிடம் / மிகச்சிறிய
mirror	-	muhakkanhnhaadi	- முகக்கண்ணாடி
moon	-	santhiran	- சந்திரன்
mosquito	-	nulampu / kosu	- நுளம்பு / கொசு
moustache	-	meesai	- மீசை
mud	-	chehru	- சேறு

N

naughty	-	kuzhappadi / suddi	குழப்படி / - சுட்டி
necklace	- kaluththu maalai	-	கழுத்துமாலை
net	-	valai	- வலை
number	-	ilakkam	- இலக்கம்
nurse	-	thaathi	- தாதி

O

obey	-	kiizhpadi	- கீழ்ப்படி
ocean	-	samuththiram	- சமுத்திரம்
offence	-	kuttram	- குற்றம்
oil	-	enhnhai	- எண்ணெய்
old	-	pazhaiya	- பழைய
	-	vayathaana	- வயதான
once	-	orumurai	- ஒருமுறை
only	-	oreh oru	- ஒரேஒரு /

		thaniya		தனிய
ooze	-	kasi	-	கசி
or	-	allathu	-	அல்லது
original	-	muulam	-	மூலம்

P

peace	-	samaathaanam	-	சமாதானம்
percent	-	satha veetham	-	சதவீதம்
press	-	amaththu	-	அமத்து
province	-	maahaanham	-	மாகாணம்
part	-	pahuthi	-	பகுதி
partner	-	pankaali	-	பங்காளி
		thunhai	-	துணை
partnership	-	kuuddumuyatchi	-	கூட்டுமுயற்சி
patient	-	nohyaalli	-	நோயாளி
patience	-	porrumai	-	பொறுமை
peel	-	uti	-	உரி
pure	-	thuuya	-	தூய

Q

queen	-	arasi	-	அரசி
quick	-	kethiyaai / viraivaai	-	கெதியாய் / விரைவாய்
quiet	-	amaithi	-	அமைதி
quit	-	kaali-sei	-	காலிசெய்

R

rag	-	kanthai	-	கந்தை	
railway	-	irayil-paathai	-	இரயில்பாதை	
raise	-	thooku	-	தூக்கு	
		uyarththu	-	உயர்த்து	
remember	-	ninaivu /	-	நினைவு /	
	-	gnapaham,		ஞாபகம்	
rich	-	panhakkaara	-	பணக்கார	
river	-	aaru	-	ஆறு	
rent	-	vaadahai	-	வாடகை	

S

same	-	atheh	-	அதே
salary	-	sampalam	-	சம்பளம்
saari	-	sehlai	-	சேலை
scissors	-	kaththarikkohl	-	கத்தரிக்கோல்
secret	-	rahasium	-	ரகசியம்
send	-	anuppu	-	அனுப்பு
shoe	-	sappaaththu	-	சப்பாத்து
	-	paatha anhi	-	பாத அணி
short	-	kaddai /	-	கட்டை /
		kuruhiya		குறுகிய
snow	-	pani	-	பனி
sports	-	kehllikkai /	-	கேளிக்கை /
		villaiyaaddu		விளையாட்டு
stone	-	kal	-	கல்

sugar	-	siini	-	சீனி
sweet	-	inippu	-	இனிப்பு

T

thick	-	thadippu	-	தடிப்பு
things	-	porudka__ll__	-	பொருட்கள்
think	-	yohsi	-	யோசி
time	-	nehram	-	நேரம்
tiny	-	chinnanchiriya	-	சின்னஞ்சிறிய
truth	-	unhmai	-	உண்மை

U

ugly	-	asinkamaana	-	அசிங்கமான
umbrella	-	kudai	-	குடை
unable	-	mudiyaatha	-	முடியாத
uncertain	-	nichchayamatra-		நிச்சயமற்ற
unclean	-	asuththamaana-		அசுத்தமான
unfair	-	niyaayamatra	-	நியாயமற்ற
unfit	-	thahuthiyillai	-	தகுதியில்லை
unity	-	ottrumai	-	ஒற்றுமை
unless	-	il-laiyenil	-	இல்லையெனில்

V

vast	-	periya__ll__avaana	-	பெரியளவான
vegetable	-	marakkari	-	மரக்கறி
view	-	thohttram	-	தோற்றம்
villain	-	thiiyavan	-	தீயவன் / வில்லன்

W

wash	- kazhuvu -	கழுவு
wasp	- ku_ll_avi -	குளவி
water	- thanhnheer /	தண்ணீர்
	- neer	நீர்
way	- paathai -	பாதை
	vazhi -	வழி
weed	- ka_ll_ai -	களை
weak	- palamattra -	பலமற்ற
wind	- kattru -	காற்று

X

x-ray	- eksreh -	எக்ஸ்றே

Y

yearly	- varudaantha -	வருடாந்த
youth	- vaalipam -	வாலிபம்

Z

zebra	- varikkuthirai -	வரிக்குதிரை
zero	- puuchchiyam -	பூச்சியம்
zone	- valayam -	வலயம்

www.ingramcontent.com/pod-product-compliance
Lightning Source LLC
LaVergne TN
LVHW021817060526
838201LV00058B/3422